THE PASSION OF JESUS

A DEVOTIONAL TO CELEBRATE LENT AND
MOVE TOWARD EASTER

HOLIDAY CELEBRATION DEVOTIONALS
BOOK 2

PETER DEHAAN

The Passion of Jesus: A Devotional to Celebrate Lent and Move toward Easter

Library of Congress Control Number: 9798888090107

Published by Rock Rooster Books, Grand Rapids, Michigan

ISBNs:

- 979-8-88809-009-1 (e-book)
- 979-8-88809-010-7 (paperback)
- 979-8-88809-011-4 (hardcover)
- 979-8-88809-039-8 (audiobook)

Credits:

- Developmental editor: Julie Harbison
- Copyeditor: Robyn Mulder
- Cover design: Taryn Nergaard
- Author photo: Chelsie Jensen Photography

To Michael Roberto, for your inspiration and encouragement

Holiday Celebration Devotionals rejoice in the holidays with Jesus.

40-Day Bible Study Series takes a fresh and practical look into Scripture, book by book.

Bible Character Sketches Series celebrates people in Scripture, from the well-known to the obscure.

Visiting Churches Series takes an in-person look at church practices and traditions to inform and inspire today's followers of Jesus.

Be the first to hear about Peter's new books and receive updates at PeterDeHaan.com/updates.

CONTENTS

CELEBRATING THE PASSION OF JESUS

Many Christians and churches celebrate the season of Lent to remember Jesus and his passion for coming to earth to die for us and our sins. This is a gift to us and not something we need to earn. When we accept Jesus's present, he makes us right with Father God and reconciles us to him.

In this devotional, we'll remember the season of Lent, building up to Jesus's greatest gift to us: his death as the ultimate sin sacrifice.

Traditionally, Lent begins on Ash Wednesday and continues through to Maundy Thursday (the day before Good Friday and Jesus's death). Some church calendars, however, end Lent on Good

Friday and others on Holy Saturday. (Resurrection Sunday begins the Easter season.) Because the passion of Jesus culminates with his sacrificial death, we'll use that to conclude our devotional. This is a matter of convenience and not a theological statement or alignment with one Lenten calendar over another.

We think of Lent as lasting forty days. This parallels the forty days Jesus spends in the desert being tempted by Satan (Mark 1:12–13). This time of testing prepares Jesus for his public ministry, which culminates with his death and subsequent resurrection.

In truth, Lent spans longer than forty days. Though some church calendars tweak the details to make Lent cover forty days, let's not worry if it's longer. Regardless of the details, the purpose of Lent stays the same. During Lent we focus on Jesus and his sacrifice for us.

Depending on the year, Ash Wednesday can start as early as February 4 or as late as March 10. This is because Ash Wednesday always occurs forty-four days before Good Friday, which falls on a different date each year. Given this, we'll treat the days of Lent as building up to Good Friday, starting with Day 1 on Ash Wednesday.

We'll begin our story with Jesus's prediction that he will die—and then rise again. Following that, we'll focus on what occurs during Holy Week, starting just prior to Palm Sunday (the week before Easter). This means we'll expand the events of Jesus's last few days before his crucifixion to span most of this devotional's Lenten readings. As a result, we'll cover events prior to their appearance on the church calendar. For example, we'll cover Palm Sunday on Day 6, several weeks before its actual date on the calendar.

As we move forward, we'll give primary attention to the account in Matthew, weaving in passages from Mark, Luke, and John. This will give us a holistic perspective of the sacrificial death of our Savior.

We'll also incorporate Old Testament prophecy about the Messiah to expand our appreciation. Along the way, we'll tap into our imagination to better see things from the perspective of Jesus, his disciples, and the people he meets.

Throughout this, the goal is to consider Jesus's passion and sacrifice for us from several vantages to offer a comprehensive Lenten devotional.

The result is an inclusive meditation to remember Jesus's resolute aim to die on the cross as the ultimate sacrifice to end all sacrifices and save humanity.

May God speak to you during this Lenten season.

DAY 1, ASH WEDNESDAY: JESUS PREDICTS HIS DEATH

TODAY'S PASSAGE: MATTHEW 16:21–28, MARK 8:31–38, LUKE 9:21–26, AND JOHN 12:23–26

Focus verse: *Jesus began to explain to his disciples that he must go to Jerusalem . . . be killed and on the third day be raised to life.* (Matthew 16:21)

We open our Lenten devotional with Jesus predicting his death. This is key. It confirms that Jesus knows what will happen. His Father has a plan. Jesus agrees with the plan and moves toward it.

This means his death is intentional and he is willing to die. It's not unexpected. Jesus's purpose in coming to earth is to save us by dying for our sins—the sins of all humanity throughout all time. He will soon offer himself as the ultimate sin sacrifice to end all sin sacrifices. He knows this and tells his disciples what will soon happen.

This highlights the essential part of the passage. Jesus knows he will die.

Yet two perplexing items follow his declaration.

First, Peter objects. He pulls Jesus away from the other disciples and offers correction. He wants Jesus to live and doesn't understand that the Messiah must die. Jesus's response shocks us.

He says, "Get behind me, Satan."

Is he calling Peter Satan? Is Satan controlling Peter? Possibly. But an alternate understanding is that Peter speaks from his human perspective. Satan tries to use the disciple's words to attack Jesus. The enemy desires to cast doubt into Jesus's mind, cause him to question his mission, and consider a non-lethal alternative.

So, when Jesus says, "Get behind me, Satan," he addresses the accuser. We can do the same.

The other confusing statement happens next. Jesus says that anyone who wants to be his disciple should pick up his cross and follow him. What does he mean to pick up our cross to follow him?

Jesus has said he will die and then overcome death. We know that in doing so, he dies so that we will live.

Yet, if we follow him, we need to be likewise ready to die for our faith, to die for him. Figuratively, we are to pick up our cross—the Roman tool for death. Most of us won't need to die for Jesus, but we must be willing to do so if the situation calls for it.

This means we must adopt a spiritual point of view to replace our human perspective. We need to exchange our worldly outlook with an eternal expectation. Our life here on earth means nothing compared to our life eternal with Jesus. We prove we understand this when we pick up our cross to follow him.

We don't need to be willing to die for Jesus before he will save us. Instead, our willingness to die is in response to him saving us.

Questions: *What do we do when we face temptation? What must we change to best pick up our cross and follow Jesus?*

Prayer: Jesus, may we live a life worthy of you and your call to follow you.

DAY 2, THURSDAY: THE VOICE OF GOD

TODAY'S PASSAGE: MATTHEW 17:1–9, MARK 9:1–9, LUKE 9:28–36, AND JOHN 12:27–30

Focus verse: *"This is my Son, whom I love; with him I am well pleased. Listen to him!"* (Matthew 17:5)

Yesterday's passage ended with the puzzling statement that "some of you present won't experience death before you see me coming in my kingdom" (Matthew 16:28). What follows this is an event we call the transfiguration, implicitly fulfilling Jesus's cryptic prediction. Peter, James, and John are there to see his supernatural transformation.

The three disciples ascend a mountain with Jesus. Suddenly his face shines—his countenance transfigures. This means his appearance changes; it's glorified. Moses and Elijah appear. They talk with Jesus.

Peter wants to commemorate this unprecedented event—Jesus's transfiguration and two dead patriarchs appearing before them. He offers to build them each a shrine or tabernacle in their honor. Before Jesus can respond, a bright cloud forms.

The voice of Father God comes from the cloud. "This is my Son," he says. "I love him and am pleased with him. Listen to what he says."

In one succinct declaration, God confirms Jesus as the Son of God, affirms Jesus's ministry, and commands the disciples to listen to him.

Does hearing God's audible voice about Jesus sound familiar?

Three years earlier, before Jesus begins his public ministry, he asks John the Baptizer to baptize him—even though the sinless Jesus has no sins to repent from. When Jesus comes out of the water, three astonishing things happen.

First, heaven opens, revealing a glimpse into the spiritual realm. What do the people see? What awe-inspiring sights confront them?

Next, the Spirit of God descends from heaven,

looking like a dove. Imagine the time it takes for the form to travel the distance from heaven to earth. It isn't instantaneous. It gets their attention. The people have never seen anything like it. They're astounded by this unique event. The dove lands on Jesus, showing his connection with heaven, his divine bond with the godhead.

A voice from heaven calls out. "This is my Son," God says. "I love him and am pleased with him" (Matthew 3:13–17). This is almost identical to what God says at the transfiguration. This time the Father, Son, and Holy Spirit are all present. We see the triune God at work.

Two times God speaks audibly about Jesus. The first time is to prepare for him to begin his earthly ministry. The second time is in preparation for him to conclude it. He'll do this by dying for our sins, rising from the dead, and returning to heaven.

Both times Father God confirms his Son and affirms Jesus's ministry.

Questions: *How does God speak to us today? How well do we do at listening to the words of Jesus, as the Father instructed?*

Prayer: Father God, may we always hear your voice and obey your words.

DAY 3, FRIDAY: JESUS AGAIN
PREDICTS HIS DEATH

TODAY'S PASSAGE: MATTHEW 20:17–19, MARK
10:32–34, AND LUKE 18:31–34

Focus verse: *"On the third day he will be raised to life!"*
(Matthew 20:19)

In the reading for Day 1 we covered Jesus predicting his death and resurrection. This isn't the only time he says this. He does it again . . . and again.

The second time is much like the first. They're in Galilee. Jesus tells his disciples three things.

First, he will be delivered over to the hands of men. This is cryptic, but we now know that this means Judas will betray him to the Jewish leaders who will arrest him.

Jesus's other two statements are clear. They will kill him, and he will arise to life (Matthew 17:22–23, Mark 9:30–32, and Luke 9:43–45).

This time Peter keeps quiet. He may have learned from his prior impetuous outburst that saying nothing is the wise action. Even so, the disciples react strongly.

Matthew says they're filled with grief. This suggests they rightly hear the dying part but miss the rising part. Though Jesus raised some people from the dead, the disciples are much more familiar with death than resurrection.

In contrast to Matthew's account, Mark and Luke say the disciples don't understand what he means but are afraid to ask for clarification.

Which is it? It's both. Combining these, we see the disciples are concerned because they don't understand.

This is the second time Jesus predicts his death.

The third time Jesus predicts his death is on their way to Jerusalem. This time he gives more details.

He says he'll be handed over to the religious leaders. They'll condemn him to death and hand him over to the Gentiles—that is, non-Jews, implying the Romans. (This is because the Jews lack the authority to execute anyone, but the Romans can.) The Romans will mock Jesus, flog him, and execute him by crucifixion.

But his death isn't the end. Three days later, he will rise again to life. Though Matthew and Mark don't record the disciples' reaction, Luke does. He says they don't understand any of what Jesus said.

Why do Matthew, Mark, and Luke all tell us that Jesus three times predicts his death?

It may be for emphasis, or it may be to make sure we don't miss his prediction. But the repetition may harken back to the Old Testament law that requires two or three witnesses to condemn a man to death (Deuteronomy 17:6). Though Jesus isn't supplying three witnesses, he does state three times that he'll be condemned to die.

It's as if he's telling his disciples that he knows he will die and accepts it.

Questions: *When has grief filled us over something we didn't understand? When has God needed to repeat his message to us before we understood his instruction?*

Prayer: Heavenly Father, may we understand what you say to us in Scripture and through your Holy Spirit.

DAY 4, SATURDAY: LAZARUS

TODAY'S PASSAGE: JOHN 11:1–44

Focus verse: *Jesus called in a loud voice, "Lazarus, come out!" The dead man came out, his hands and feet wrapped with strips of linen, and a cloth around his face.* (John 11:43–44)

The Bible tells us about three siblings: Martha, Mary, and Lazarus. Yet Matthew and Mark don't mention them at all. Only Luke and John tell us about Martha and Mary, while Lazarus only shows up in John, chapters 11 and 12. (Though Luke records a parable about a man named Lazarus, he's a different person.)

John says that Jesus loves Martha, Mary, and Lazarus. Though our Savior loves everyone, Scripture seldom names them, but it does specify Martha, Mary, and Lazarus. This should get our attention as to how important they are to Jesus.

In today's account, Lazarus is sick. Sick enough for the sisters to worry. They send word to Jesus. They don't ask for him to come heal their brother, but merely state that he's ill.

Knowing what will happen, Jesus says Lazarus's illness will not end in death but in glory to Father God and his Son. But he does nothing for two days.

In a delightful exchange, Jesus tells his disciples that Lazarus is sleeping, and Jesus will go wake him. The disciples take this literally, but Jesus means it figuratively. In truth, Lazarus is dead. Jesus uses the euphemism to *wake him* to mean resurrect him. The implication is that, to Jesus, raising someone from the dead is no harder than for us to wake someone from a deep sleep. So it will be with us when we die. Jesus will wake us to live with him in paradise forever.

Jesus heads for Bethany, where the siblings live. He arrives to find that Lazarus is four-days dead and buried. Both Martha and Mary have confidence that Jesus had the power to heal their brother and prevent his death. And Martha has faith that her brother will one day rise again. But neither sister expects Jesus to do anything for their dead brother now.

Jesus goes to Lazarus's tomb. Martha, Mary, and the many Jews mourning with them follow. When he arrives, he instructs them to remove the large stone that blocks the entrance. He thanks Papa for hearing his prayer and commands Lazarus to come out of his tomb.

To everyone's amazement, Lazarus hobbles forth, still wrapped in his burial cloths. It's a miracle of miracles. Though this isn't the first time Jesus raises someone from the dead, this is the most spectacular one—and the most memorable. Many people witness Lazarus's resurrection, creating quite a stir, which we'll cover in a few days.

In the end, Lazarus doesn't die, and God and his Son receives glory.

Questions: *How well do we do to accept that Jesus loves us? What do we think about Jesus raising someone from the dead?*

Prayer: Father God, may our lives—and death—give you glory.

DAY 5, SUNDAY: BORROWING A DONKEY FOR JESUS

TODAY'S PASSAGE: MATTHEW 21:1–6, MARK 11:1–10, AND LUKE 19:28–34

Focus verse: *"Go to the village ahead of you, and at once you will find a donkey tied there, with her colt by her. Untie them and bring them to me."* (Matthew 21:2)

As Jesus and his followers approach Jerusalem, he sends two of his disciples on a mission. He sends them to borrow a donkey and its colt. Though they don't know the reason for this request, he plans to ride the colt into Jerusalem. This will fulfill the Old Testament prophecy that the king will come to them—righteous and victorious—riding the foal of a donkey (Zechariah 9:9).

Jesus doesn't tell the pair to seek the owner and

ask permission first, which seems like the proper thing to do. Instead, he tells them what to say if questioned. This implies they will, in fact, be stopped and quizzed.

When we consider this request in a modern context, what he asks them to do is even more astounding. It would be like Jesus telling us to take someone's bicycle or even a car. Certainly, this would be a risky thing to do, as we could be arrested and prosecuted for stealing—for taking what isn't ours. I'd certainly balk at Jesus's instruction. I'm not sure I'd be willing to break the law for him.

As for his disciples, they don't question him. They obey. They are, however, no doubt familiar with the Old Testament law that stipulates the punishment for taking someone's donkey. The penalty is to pay back double, to make a two-fold restitution for having a stolen donkey (Exodus 22:4) or being in the illegal possession of one (Exodus 22:9). They are to not even covet—that is, to want —it (Exodus 20:17).

Although Mark and Luke say that Jesus tells them to take the colt, Matthew notes that Jesus tells them to take both the donkey *and* her colt. This makes sense. The donkey is trained and will go wherever they lead her, with the colt following along. But the colt alone may fight them for trying to separate it from its mother. So, in this case, they take two donkeys, which would require a restitution of four animals.

Yet, the disciples do as Jesus instructed. And they do so without question or hesitation.

Mark and Luke both mention that people nearby question what the disciples are doing. I suspect they know who owns the pair of animals— and it isn't the disciples. But the disciples don't explain. They say what Jesus tells them to say. "The Lord needs them and will send them back shortly."

The people accept this.

Questions: *What does the Lord need us to do? What is our response when God tells us to do something that makes no sense or is even illegal?*

Prayer: Lord, may we hear you, listen, and obey— in all situations and at all times.

DAY 6, MONDAY: THE TRIUMPHAL ENTRY

TODAY'S PASSAGE: MATTHEW 21:7–11, MARK 11:7–11, LUKE 19:35–38, AND JOHN 12:12–16

Focus verse: *The crowds that went ahead of him and those that followed shouted, "Hosanna to the Son of David!"* (Matthew 21:9)

Having secured the colt for him to ride, the disciples lay their coats on the donkey as a makeshift saddle for Jesus. Mark and Luke tell us that no one had ever ridden the colt. Therefore, the animal has never carried anything on its back and would instinctively buck if someone tried to mount it. Yet Jesus climbs on with no problem.

As Jesus rides into Jerusalem, the people spread

their coats on the road, a traditional gesture worthy of a king (see 2 Kings 9:13). Those without a coat cut branches to lie in the road (see Leviticus 23:40). Only John says these branches are from palm trees. Even so, we call Jesus's triumphal arrival Palm Sunday.

Jesus's grand entry into Jerusalem parallels that of a victorious king returning from battle, riding on a donkey, which signifies him coming in peace. Jesus likewise rides into Jerusalem. The people hail him as their king.

They call out their praises to Jesus. "Hosanna to the Son of David!"

Though we now think of *hosanna* as proclaiming praise, the word means "save," as in "save us" or "Lord, save us" (see Psalm 118:25).

The people see Jesus as their Savior. However, they perceive him as a physical savior, a military hero who will rescue them from Roman oppression. They don't understand he is a spiritual savior who will rescue them from sin's oppression.

"Blessed is he who comes in the Lord's name," they shout (see Psalm 118:26). "Hosanna in the highest heaven."

Mark gives us a fourth line: "Blessed is the

coming kingdom of our father David!" While Luke adds, "Peace in heaven and glory in the highest!"

As this grand procession approaches Jerusalem, they create quite a stir. This grabs the people's attention. They ask in amazement, "Who is this?"

The throng responds, "This is Jesus, the prophet from Nazareth in Galilee" (see Deuteronomy 18:15).

Luke adds that the Pharisees implore Jesus to silence the people's adoration. He doesn't. Instead, he says that if the people keep quiet, the stones will instead cry out in praise of him (see Habakkuk 2:11).

Mark includes another detail. He says that after his triumphant entry into Jerusalem, Jesus goes to the temple courts and looks around. But since the day is late, he leaves. What he sees there, however, foreshadows what we'll cover on Day 8.

What none of the accounts mention is the two disciples returning the donkey and her colt. I'm sure they do, but confirmation would be nice.

Questions: *What have we borrowed that we need to return? How do we better trust Jesus as our Savior?*

Prayer: Jesus, may we follow you as our Savior. May our praise be as exuberant now as what we read in today's passage.

DAY 7, TUESDAY: THE JEWS' UNBELIEF

TODAY'S PASSAGE: JOHN 12:37–50

Focus verse: *Because of the Pharisees they would not openly acknowledge their faith for fear they would be put out of the synagogue.* (John 12:42)

At about this time in the book of John, we read of the Jews' response to Jesus and the miracles he performed before them. We could assume that the Jews—being immersed in the Old Testament prophecy of a coming Savior and expecting his arrival—would see Jesus as fulfilling what Scripture promised. He taught them with authority—unlike their own teachers—and drew people to him. He performed supernatural signs right in front of them. This should get their attention.

It does. But not in a positive way.

Overall, the response of the Jews is one of unbelief. How sad. Yet Isaiah predicted this with his rhetorical question, "Who has believed our message?" (Isaiah 53:1). In this, he laments both his own frustration over a lack of response to his ministry and foreshadows a future apathy for Jesus's message.

John continues with another passage from Isaiah to explain why. Although perplexing, Isaiah proclaims that God spiritually blinds the Jews' eyes so they cannot see and hardens their hearts so they cannot understand (Isaiah 6:9–10).

To understand this, let's look back at the Old Testament narrative. There we see the Jewish people as a group, as a nation, continually rejecting God and rebelling against him and his prophets. Though God is slow to anger (Exodus 34:6) and withheld his judgment generation after generation, century after century, he has at last had enough. This long-overdue punishment is spiritual blindness and hardened hearts.

Though we may be critical of God for punishing one generation for the failures of prior

The Passion of Jesus

ones, the generation of Jesus's day is no less guilty. Besides, we must remember that God is sovereign and can do whatever he wants—even if this seems unfair. Even so, Peter reminds us that God doesn't want anyone to perish (2 Peter 3:9). Hold on to this truth.

After John's discouraging passage that no one responded to Jesus's message, the apostle clarifies that some do believe. Yet they won't acknowledge their faith in Jesus in public because they fear the religious leaders will expel them from the synagogue, that is, out of their church. Nicodemus exemplifies this, coming to Jesus in secret under the anonymity of darkness (John 3:1–2).

A secret belief, however, isn't enough. Jesus himself says that we must acknowledge him before others if we expect him to acknowledge us before the Father (Matthew 10:32–33). Though Nicodemus at first feared retribution from his peers, he later makes an implicit stand for Jesus when he helps bury him, aligning himself with the Savior (John 19:39).

John doesn't mention the third category of people. They are those who believe in Jesus and aren't afraid to be with him and stand with him. All his disciples and his many followers fall into this group, yet they are a small minority.

Questions: *When have we failed to acknowledge Jesus before others? How can we do better next time?*

Prayer: Lord Jesus, may we stand up for you, especially when it's hard to do.

DAY 8, WEDNESDAY: JESUS CLEARS THE TEMPLE COURTS

TODAY'S PASSAGE: MATTHEW 21:12–13, MARK 11:15–17, AND LUKE 19:45–46

Focus verse: *"It is written," [Jesus] said to them, "'My house will be called a house of prayer,' but you are making it 'a den of robbers.'"* (Matthew 21:13)

After Jesus rides into Jerusalem on the colt, he goes to the temple courts. This is the area that surrounds the actual temple. People must go through the court to reach the temple. He looks at what's happening. Though Matthew and Luke don't include this detail, Mark says Jesus leaves because it's late. He returns the next day.

Jesus isn't pleased at what he sees happening in the temple. In fact, he's downright angry. He flips over the tables of the money changers and the benches of those selling doves. He creates quite a scene. Quoting from the Bible, Jesus says, "My house will be called a place for prayer" (Isaiah 56:7), but you turned it into "a den of robbers" (Jeremiah 7:11).

Both groups of merchants are present to aid in worship. This is because some ceremonies require sacrificing a dove. Instead of traveling—sometimes a great distance—with a dove, the people buy one when they reach the temple. And because they might hold a different currency, they need to exchange their money for the right form before making their purchase.

Though we can assume these groups of merchants make an exorbitant profit by preying on those who show up on their pilgrimage, this isn't likely Jesus's concern. His issue is that they bring their business into the temple courts when they should have set up shop outside.

Instead of keeping the temple and court reserved for worship, we can imagine the temple leaders allowing this to happen. They may have even accepted a kickback to permit it. In doing so, God's house of prayer becomes a haven for robbers.

Though I don't advocate anyone doing this—in

fact, *don't* do this—let's use our imaginations a bit. Consider your Sunday church service. Crowds of people move about. Excitement builds for the service about to begin. Worshipful music plays in the background. Suddenly a man yells. He flips over displays that hold materials for the service. The crazed man chases away the people staffing the tables. He spouts Scripture.

It would make quite a scene.

This is what Jesus does. Though he gets the people's attention, do his actions cause them to stop what they're doing?

I think not.

This isn't the first time Jesus does this, but the second.

The first time happened three years earlier (John 2:13–17). It's when Jesus starts his ministry, right after performing his first public miracle at the wedding in Cana.

Besides doves in the temple courts, there are also cattle and sheep there. That means there are also droppings. It's hard for me to imagine piles of animal waste in the temple courts, but where there are animals, there's going to be manure.

This time Jesus makes a whip. He overturns tables, money scatters, frightened animals flee, and people try to escape his wrath. Zeal consumes him (Psalm 69:9).

Yet, three years later, they're back. And Jesus goes after them again.

Questions: *What do we do in our church services that might need reforming? When have we let commerce interfere with worship?*

Prayer: Jesus, may we have your zeal for the things that matter to you and the wisdom to temper our passion for everything else.

DAY 9, THURSDAY: PLOTTING AGAINST JESUS

TODAY'S PASSAGE: MATTHEW 21:14–17, MARK 11:18–19, AND LUKE 19:47–48

Focus verse: *The chief priests and the teachers of the law heard this and began looking for a way to kill him.*
(Mark 11:18)

A fter Jesus clears the merchants from the courtyard around the temple, people come to him for healing. This includes the blind and the lame. And Jesus heals them.

Take a moment to consider this—not that Jesus heals those who hurt, which is an amazing feat we must not overlook—but where he is.

He's at the temple. He just drove away the merchants from this exact place. Even though they were there to facilitate worship, they disgraced the temple and detracted from the prayers people came to offer.

But this doesn't stop Jesus from healing people there. As he cures them, the children shout their praise, "Hosanna to the Son of David!" This continues the chants of the crowd that occurred when Jesus rode into Jerusalem (Day 6).

Healing people is another action that goes beyond the original purpose of the temple. But Jesus is doing good. He serves these people in need and improves their lives. What better place to do this than at the temple? (See Luke 6:9.) In addition to healing them there, he also teaches.

The religious hierarchy—the leading priests and Bible teachers—should be happy to see the bodies of the infirmed made whole and hear truth proclaimed.

They are not.

They criticize the children for their joyful noise (see Psalm 98:4). Jesus responds by quoting Scripture about children offering their praise (Psalm 8:2).

Mark and Luke both say that the religious leaders want to kill him for what he's doing.

Matthew mentions this also but in other passages (Matthew 12:14 and Matthew 26:3–5).

The religious leaders scheme for a way to kill Jesus. They don't care that he heals people or teaches them about God. By doing this, he threatens their way of life. They don't see God's hand at work in fulfilling the Old Testament law and prophetic messages.

Their solution is to get rid of Jesus, even if they must kill him.

Over the past two thousand years, Christians have reacted the same way to other Jesus followers they disagree with. In the extreme, Christians have killed other Christians in the name of their religion. They want to perpetuate what they know, what they love, not caring that others may have an equally good—or even better and more God-honoring—approach.

May we not follow their error.

Questions: *What must we change about our time at church to do good and help others? When have we fought to keep the status quo instead of embracing what God is doing?*

Prayer: Lord, may we do good for you and seek ways to advance your kingdom, even if it makes us uncomfortable.

DAY 10, FRIDAY: THE FIG TREE DIES

TODAY'S PASSAGE: MATTHEW 21:18–22 AND
MARK 11:12–14, 20–25

Focus verse: *"If you believe, you will receive whatever you ask for in prayer."* (Matthew 21:22)

The next morning, as Jesus and his troop return to Jerusalem, he's hungry. Seeing a fig tree, he expects a tasty meal and searches for fruit. Though the tree has lots of leaves, there is no fruit. He curses it, and it at once withers.

Mark's account is slightly different. He says it's not until the next day when the tree has shriveled up and died.

If this minor discrepancy bothers you, here's a thought to consider. It's the point of view of the disciples, with them not all seeing the same thing at the same time.

Though they all hear Jesus curse the tree, only half see what happens. They watch the tree shrivel up and die. The others are impatient and continue their journey, not waiting to watch what occurs. It's not until the next day that they see the outcome of Jesus's words. Hence, we have two accounts, depending on which disciple we ask.

And if you're bothered that Jesus killed the unproductive fig tree, consider one of his parables. In this story, another unproductive fig tree receives one more year to produce. If it does not, the gardener will cut it down (Luke 13:6–9). We should take this parable as a solemn reminder to produce spiritual fruit for Jesus.

Regardless, this detail of when the fig tree dies isn't important. Yes, the power of Jesus's words that condemned the tree should amaze us. But his teaching that follows this miracle should amaze us even more.

He says that if we have faith and don't doubt, we can command a mountain to move into the sea. And it will happen. Paul later calls this "a faith that can move mountains" (1 Corinthians 13:2).

"If you believe," Jesus says, "you will receive whatever you ask for in prayer."

Mark's passage gives us more of Jesus's teaching about this. He says that whatever we ask in prayer, if we believe we have received it, it will happen.

I don't yet have a faith that will move mountains —or instantaneously kill fig trees—and I don't know anyone who does. But we can exercise our faith in smaller areas, praying without doubt for the impossible, and it will happen.

Questions: *If receiving these kinds of answers to our prayers seems unfathomable, who can we align with to model it for us and teach us? We may not have faith that can move mountains, but what level of faith do we have?*

Prayer: Heavenly Father, show us how to pray in faith and receive the answers to our prayers.

DAY 11, SATURDAY: JESUS'S AUTHORITY QUESTIONED

TODAY'S PASSAGE: MATTHEW 21:23–27, MARK 11:27–33, AND LUKE 20:1–8

Focus verse: *"By what authority are you doing these things?" [the religious leaders] asked. "And who gave you this authority?"* (Matthew 21:23)

L et's recap what Jesus has done in the past few hours.

First, he rides into Jerusalem like a victorious king, with the people shouting their praises to him. This continues despite the protests of the religious leaders.

Next, he drives the merchants out of the temple courts, making quite a scene, which disturbs the religious activities there.

After that, he heals people, including the lame and the blind.

And he teaches.

He does these last three things at the temple.

All this upsets the religious leaders. Growing tired of Jesus and his disruption to their sacred practices and established way of life, they challenge him.

"By whose authority do you do these things?" they ask.

From a human perspective, they view themselves as the only ones who can grant such authority. Since they know they haven't done this, they reason that his only response is to admit he acts on his own accord. Then they can tell him to stop.

Jesus sees their duplicity and counters it. He says he'll answer their question once they answer his. "Did God give John authority to preach and baptize, or did he act on his own?"

The religious leaders realize that if they say God, they condemn themselves for rejecting John as God's messenger. Yet if they say John acted alone, the people will rise against them because they view John as God's prophet.

With neither answer acceptable, they say, "We don't know."

Based on their non-answer, Jesus declines to respond to their question.

Having already implied he is greater than John (Matthew 11:10–11), Jesus could have asked them the same question about himself: "Does God give me authority to preach and baptize, or am I acting on my own?"

If they answer "God," they even more so condemn themselves. Yet if they claim Jesus acts on his own, the people are even more likely to rise to his defense.

Yet there's more to this question of Jesus's authority, which Matthew has already covered.

First, the crowds realize he teaches with authority, much unlike the other religious teachers (Matthew 7:28–29). These are the very ones criticizing him.

Next, Jesus proves he has authority to forgive sins by healing a paralyzed man (Matthew 9:6–8).

Then he delegates his authority to his disciples before sending them to cast out evil spirits and heal people (Matthew 10:1). And he'll do this a second time right before he returns to heaven (Matthew 28:18–20).

Jesus has God's authority and uses that authority, but the religious leaders are so focused on themselves, and what they wrongly assume about God, that they miss it—and oppose God in the process (see Acts 5:38–39).

Questions: *When have we opposed God by our actions, words, or practices? When God tells us to do something, do we obey or seek human permission (authority)?*

Prayer: Father God, may we act under your authority and not seek human permission to do your will.

DAY 12, SUNDAY: THE PHARISEES TAKE OFFENSE

TODAY'S PASSAGE: MATTHEW 21:28–46, MARK 12:12, AND LUKE 20:9–19

Focus verse: *When the chief priests and the Pharisees heard Jesus' parables, they knew he was talking about them.* (Matthew 21:45)

I mmediately after Jesus counters the religious leaders who challenge his authority, he shares some parables. With a crowd already gathered, it provides him with a perfect time to teach.

Matthew records three of these stories. We call them the parable of the two sons, the parable of the tenants, and the parable of the wedding banquet (Matthew 21:28–22:14). Mark and Luke focus on the middle one of the three, the parable of the tenants.

In this parable, Jesus tells of a wealthy man who plants a vineyard and prepares it for use. He rents it to farmers and moves away. At harvest time, he sends his representatives to collect his share of the crop from the tenants.

The farmers mistreat the envoys. They beat one, kill a second, and stone a third. The landowner sends even more servants, but they receive the same ill treatment. At last, he sends his son, expecting the tenants to respect him. They don't.

The evil farmers reason that if they kill the heir, they can seize his inheritance. So they murder him.

Jesus asks the crowd, "What will the landowner do?"

"He'll bring those bad tenants to justice," the people say, "and rent the vineyard to others, who will pay him what they owe."

Jesus ties the parable into Scripture, which says that the stone the builders rejected has become the cornerstone, and the people marveled that God did this (Psalm 118:22–23).

How do the parable and the psalm connect?

The landowner's son represents Jesus, whom most of the people will reject and kill. Yet God has made him a cornerstone.

Though we typically think of a cornerstone as a

commemorative part of a building, historically it serves a functional purpose. It lies at the corner of two intersecting walls, establishing the basis for the two sides of the building. Without a properly set cornerstone, the structural integrity of the building is in doubt, leaving it unstable.

Though rejected by the tenants, God made Jesus the cornerstone of our faith.

The religious leaders and Pharisees realize Jesus's parable is about them. They know they're the evil tenants in his story. And if they take time to consider his teaching more fully, they'll see it as a prediction that they'll also kill him.

Instead, they're offended and look for a way to arrest him without causing a riot.

Questions: *When have Jesus's words offended us? Have we made Jesus the cornerstone of our lives?*

Prayer: Jesus, when the Bible tells us what we don't want to hear, may we not take offense and instead respond as good tenants.

DAY 13, MONDAY: THE GREATEST COMMANDMENT

TODAY'S PASSAGE: MATTHEW 22:34–40 AND MARK 12:28–34

Focus verse: *"'Love the Lord your God with all your heart and with all your soul and with all your mind.' This is the first and greatest commandment."* (Matthew 22:37)

After he shares the three parables, the religious leaders—roiling over Jesus's parable of the tenants—seek to trap him into saying something they can use against him. Remember, they want to arrest him but are afraid because he has so much public support. Discrediting him is their best option—at this time.

First come the Pharisees. After flattering him, they ask if it's right to pay taxes. Jesus's delightful answer tells them to "give back to Caesar what is Caesar's, and to God what is God's" (Matthew 22:15–22).

With the Pharisees' failure, the Sadducees take a turn. They wonder if our resurrected forms will marry. It's an interesting choice, since the Sadducees don't believe in the resurrection of the dead. Jesus puts them in their place, too, astonishing the crowd in the process (Matthew 22:23–33).

After this, the Pharisees and Sadducees conspire to form a new strategy. They send an expert in the law (today, we might call him a theologian) to Jesus. The man asks Jesus, "What is the greatest commandment?"

This is a question everyone must want to know. The Jews followed tens of thousands of rules. It's a mind-numbing list of dos and don'ts.

They developed these rules over time to guide them in their daily interactions, expounding on the original 613 laws Moses gave to the people. This occurred after they left Egypt for the land God promised to give them.

Drilling down further from these 613 laws are the ten big ones, which we call the Ten Commandments.

Now Jesus must pick one as the greatest of all.

The greatest commandment, Jesus says, is to love God far more than anything else. Specifically, to do so with all our heart, soul, and strength (Deuteronomy 6:5).

But Jesus is quick to tack on a second one. (Isn't this just like Jesus, to not do what the people expect?) The second-greatest command is to love others as much as we love ourselves (Leviticus 19:18).

Everything else in Scripture flows from these two commands.

Think about it.

Of the Ten Commandments, the first four are about our relationship with God, that is, loving *him*. The last six are about our relationship with others, that is, loving *them*.

Also, looking at all 613 of the laws Moses gave, we can see that they all boil down to these two commandments.

We are to love God and love others. When we do this, everything else will take care of itself.

Questions: *How well do we do at loving God? How well do we do at loving others?*

Prayer: Lord, may we love you to the grand extent you desire. And may we love others as much as we love ourselves.

DAY 14, TUESDAY: WHOSE SON IS THE CHRIST?

TODAY'S PASSAGE: MATTHEW 22:41–46, MARK 12:35–37, AND LUKE 20:41–44

Focus verse: *No one could say a word in reply, and from that day on no one dared to ask him any more questions.*
(Matthew 22:46)

H aving deftly deflected all three of their ploys, Jesus now has a question for his detractors. "Considering the Messiah," he asks, "whose son is he?"

"The son of David," they answer (see Matthew 1:6–16).

Then Jesus quotes one of David's psalms: "The Lord said to my Lord: 'Sit at my right hand until I put your enemies under your feet'" (Psalm 110:1).

"If David calls him Lord," Jesus asks, "how can he be his son?"

How indeed? No one has an answer and from that moment on, they don't harass him with any more questions to trap him.

Jesus's response from Psalms has always confounded me. This is because the passage repeats the word *Lord*. Yes, the first says *the* Lord, and the second says *my* Lord, implying a distinction. And knowing the dictionary says *Lord* can mean either God or Jesus helps a little, but not enough.

Those who know Hebrew tell me that two different Hebrew words appear in this passage, with them both translated as *Lord*. Therefore, the source of my confusion is not the holy text but the English language.

Though most versions of the Bible use *Lord* twice in this passage, not all do.

Some replace the first *Lord* with *Yahweh* (LEB, NOG, and WEB), *Jehovah* (DARBY and YLT), Adoni (OJB and TLV), or *Eternal* (VOICE).

Others replace the second *Lord* with *Messiah* (TLB) or *Master* (ICB).

What helps me the most, however, is the Amplified Bible, which reads, "The Lord (Father) says to my Lord (the Messiah, His Son) . . ."

From all this, we see Jesus as the Son of God *and* the son of David, that is, David's descendant. Jesus is also the son of Mary and Joseph.

But there's more.

We're part of God's family too. At least we are when we follow Jesus. As followers of the Christ, his Father adopts us into his family as sons and daughters (Romans 8:15, Galatians 4:4–5, and Ephesians 1:4–6). This makes us children of God. We are part of his family. We are his children. This makes us heirs of God and co-heirs with Jesus (Romans 8:17), poised to receive our inheritance from him (Colossians 1:12 and 1 Peter 1:3–4).

Adoption is one explanation of how we become part of God's family. Another is marriage.

In Revelation we read that we—who are collectively Jesus's church—will one day marry him. In this, we picture Jesus as the groom and the church is his pure, spotless bride (Revelation 19:6–9). In considering this, push aside the thought of a sexual union and replace the image with a spiritual intimacy. When we marry the Lamb, we marry into the family and become a child of God.

Jesus is the son of God and we—as his church—are children of God, through both adoption and marriage.

Questions: *How well do we do at considering ourselves a child of God? What is our reaction at the thought of being married to Jesus?*

Prayer: Thank you, Father God, that we are your sons and daughters, children of the king.

DAY 15, WEDNESDAY: BE READY
TODAY'S PASSAGE: MATTHEW 24:1–44, MARK 13, AND LUKE 21:5–38

Focus verse: *"But about that day or hour no one knows, not even the angels in heaven, nor the Son, but only the Father.* (Matthew 24:36)

After Jesus does some more teaching (Matthew 23), he and his disciples leave the temple. What a day they've had. In the last few hours, they've seen praise from the crowds, verbal sparring with the religious leaders, miracles, and more brilliant teaching. I'm sure they're all looking forward to a good night's rest to prepare them for whatever lies ahead.

But Jesus is always looking for a teachable moment, and one occurs when his disciples point to the temple with its impressive stones and gifts dedicated to God, along with all the other surrounding buildings.

History tells us that this rebuilt and refurbished temple was much grander than the original version first constructed by King Solomon—as detailed in the Bible—or the more modest reconstruction centuries later by Zerubbabel. This version looms as a most impressive sight. This is the temple and temple area that his disciples point out and that Jesus talks about.

With all the disciples focused on the impressive worship space, Jesus seizes the moment. "Look at all this," he says. "It will all be destroyed, with not one stone left standing."

Let that sink in. The disciples do.

It's not until later that evening—once they retreat to the Mount of Olives—that they ask him for an explanation.

"Let nobody trick you," he says. "You'll hear false claims that I've returned. There will be wars, rumors of wars, famines, and earthquakes. But this is only the start of the end and not the end."

Jesus continues, giving a detailed—and disturbing—explanation about what will occur. We see some of these things happening today. This leads many to assume the end is near, that the end of life as we know it could happen at any moment. Never mind that most of Jesus's followers have reached the same conclusion in each generation over the past two thousand years.

Regardless, Jesus confirms no one knows when the end will occur, not the angels in heaven, not even him. Only Father God knows the exact timing,

Why does Jesus tell us what will happen if we can't know when it will occur?

So that we'll be on the lookout, living in expectation that he could return at any moment. This isn't an excuse to coast through the rest of our lives. Instead, it's an imperative call to leave nothing for tomorrow, but to do all we can for him and his kingdom today.

Then we will be ready for him when he comes back for us.

Questions: Are we watching and ready for Jesus's return? What have we put off that we should do for him today?

Prayer: Jesus, may you find us watching, waiting, and ready for your return.

DAY 16, THURSDAY: WELL DONE
TODAY'S PASSAGE: MATTHEW 24:45–25:46

Focus verse: *"Well done, good and faithful servant!"*
(Matthew 25:21)

As Jesus winds down his teaching about the end times and his return, he shares an example of two servants. One is faithful and wise. The other is wicked. The first does what's expected by his master—he'll be ready whenever the master comes back—while the second treats those in his charge badly and goes out drinking. When his master arrives unexpectedly, he exacts eternal punishment on the wicked servant.

May Jesus find us doing what we should be doing when he returns and not goofing off.

To make sure we understand, Jesus gives two parables.

The first is about ten virgins waiting to celebrate a wedding. Though they know the event will happen, they don't know when. Each one has an oil lamp. Each one has filled her lamp with oil, but five also brought an extra jar of fuel. They've planned and are wise. The others lack foresight and are foolish.

In the middle of the night—when they least expect it—they hear the groom is on his way. They arise and trim their lamps. This means they adjust them from a dim, barely lit state to full brightness. They all realize their lamps are about out of oil. The wise ones add fuel from their reserves. The foolish ones can't and go to buy more oil.

That's when the groom arrives. The five wise ones are waiting and go in for a massive celebration. He shuts the doors. When the foolish ones get back, the groom won't let them in. They weren't ready for his return, and it's too late. They missed out.

This parable reminds us to be ready for Jesus.

The second parable is about talents (bags of gold). A man preparing to embark on a journey entrusts some of his money to his servants: five talents to one, two to another, and one to a third. (According to a footnote in the NIV, a talent is worth about twenty years of a day labor's wage.)

When he returns, he calls them each to give an account. The first and second were both productive and doubled their money. "Well done, good and faithful servant," he says. "Join me in my happiness."

The third servant was lazy and hid the money. He didn't even bother to deposit the funds in a bank to earn interest. The master takes the servant's one talent and gives it to the one who has ten. He throws the slothful servant into darkness to receive judgment.

This parable reminds us to be productive for Jesus.

Jesus concludes with an example of a shepherd separating his sheep from his goats. This is analogous to Jesus judging people when he returns. Some served him well, receiving an eternal reward. Those who didn't serve him well will receive eternal punishment.

May we serve Jesus well.

Questions: *What are we doing to be ready for Jesus's return? What are we doing to be productive for him?*

Prayer: Jesus, may we live lives worthy of you as your faithful and wise servants.

DAY 17, FRIDAY: SCHEMING TO KILL JESUS

TODAY'S PASSAGE: MATTHEW 26:1–5, MARK 14:1–2, AND JOHN 11:45–57

Focus verse: *[The religious leaders] schemed to arrest Jesus secretly and kill him.* (Matthew 26:4)

J esus has wrapped up a lengthy teaching about the end times and his later return to earth. He shared two parables about the need for us to be ready for him to come back at any moment and the importance of being faithful and wise servants as we wait for his return.

Now he directs his attention to his disciples. He mentions the Passover is two days away, something they are all certainly aware of. He reminds them that he's going to die—something he's already told them three times (Days 1 and 3). Though he's mentioned it once before, he plainly says he'll be crucified.

The religious leaders retreat. They call a meeting to plan how they might do away with Jesus. Since he just mentioned being crucified, I wonder if this plants the idea in their minds. Though they can't legally execute anyone, Roman soldiers can. Their discussions about getting rid of Jesus may now expand to drawing the Romans into their plot. Caiaphas, the high priest, recommends that they wait until after the Passover celebration, lest the people riot.

John fills in the details. He says they call an emergency council meeting of the Sanhedrin to deal with the Jesus problem. If they don't stop him, they worry that their Roman rulers will take away their temple—their religious practices—and what little autonomous power remains for their nation. (Though the Romans reign overall and rule harshly, they allow a bit of local governance, which the Jewish leaders seek to maintain at all costs.)

The high priest, Caiaphas, speaks again. "Don't you realize that it's better for one man to die for the people than for the entire nation to perish?"

Did you catch this?

One man to die for the people is what Jesus

came to do. In saying this, Caiaphas unwittingly prophesies that Jesus will die to save the Jewish nation, as well as everyone else.

They also discuss killing Lazarus. This is because many people believe in Jesus since he raised Lazarus from the dead (John 12:9–11, 17–19). They also give an order that anyone who sees Jesus should let them know so they can arrest him.

The plans of the religious leaders oppose Jesus, seeking to permanently end his influence. But God will use their duplicity to carry out his will and Jesus's purpose. The Messiah will die so that we may live.

Jesus's death on the cross will serve as the sin sacrifice to end all sin sacrifices, making us right with Father God. This prepares us to spend eternity with them in heaven.

Questions: *When have we made a wrong decision in the name of religion or for what we believed? How have we moved on from our mistake?*

Prayer: Lord, guide our decisions to honor you and advance your kingdom.

DAY 18, SATURDAY: JESUS ANOINTED AT BETHANY

TODAY'S PASSAGE: MATTHEW 26:6–13 AND MARK 14:3–9

Focus verse: *"When she poured this perfume on my body, she did it to prepare me for burial."* (Matthew 26:12)

As we continue reading about Jesus's last week on earth before his execution, Matthew notes he is now in Bethany and not Jerusalem. This hints that Bethany is where Jesus goes each night when he leaves Jerusalem. It makes sense that he wouldn't stay in Jerusalem because it's packed with people who traveled there to take part in the annual Passover celebration.

Bible scholars say that the two cities are about two miles apart (3.2 kilometers), with the Mount of Olives and the Garden of Gethsemane near

Bethany. Bethany is also where Martha, Mary, and Lazarus live.

While in Bethany, at the home of Simon the Leper, a woman shows up with a bottle of expensive perfume. She pours it over Jesus's head as he reclines at the table.

Mark notes that the perfume is worth more than a year's wages. Pause a moment to consider using your annual income in a moment, and then it's gone. What she did is wasteful from a human standpoint but extravagant from an adoration perspective.

Jesus's disciples and others who are there criticize the waste, suggesting a better use would have been to sell the perfume and give the money to the poor. Again, consider how many people you could help and how much good you could do if you used your entire income for a year to bless them.

As is often the case, Jesus has a counter perspective.

He defends her actions, calling it a beautiful thing—a grand expression. By anointing him, she symbolically prepares his body for burial. Her actions parallel the Old Testament practice of anointing a leader (Leviticus 8:12 and 1 Samuel 10:1; also see Psalm 23:5).

Jesus predicts that history will remember her forever for what she did. Since we have this event recorded in the Bible and are still reading about it over two thousand years later, he is right.

Jesus is always right.

Questions: *What extravagant action can we take for Jesus? What can we do to help meet the needs of those who are poor and struggling? Is there a way to balance the two or make them coincide?*

Prayer: Lord, may we use what you have blessed us with to advance your kingdom and, in doing so, store up treasures in heaven.

DAY 19, SUNDAY: JUDAS AGREES TO BETRAY JESUS

TODAY'S PASSAGE: MATTHEW 26:14–16, MARK 14:10–11, AND LUKE 22:1–6

Focus verse: *"What are you willing to give me if I deliver him over to you?"* (Matthew 26:15)

Right after the woman anoints Jesus's head, preparing him for his burial, we read of Judas deciding to betray Jesus. John gives us a hint at why these two events connect.

The apostle writes that it is Judas—and not the disciples as a group or others in attendance—who objects to the waste of perfume (John 12:4–6). The explanation is that Judas is the group's treasurer, the holder of their money bag. But his concern isn't for the poor, it's for himself.

As a dishonest steward of their finances—a thief —he dips into their funds for his personal use. Had they sold the perfume, he might have been the caretaker of the proceeds. Assuming he was skimming 10 percent off the top, that means he stood to lose 10 percent of a year's wages—about five weeks of work.

Considering this, we can envision him being angry at the woman for wasting the perfume and at Jesus for defending her. To recoup some of the money he never got to see, we can guess that he decides to make Jesus pay.

Judas approaches the chief priests—some of the religious leaders. He asks how much they'll give him to deliver Jesus to them. They offer him thirty silver coins. We don't know how much they're worth, but some scholars place the value at four months of wages, though others think it's less. Regardless, Judas figures out a way to receive the money he potentially lost and perhaps much more.

We don't know if Judas thinks through the ramifications of his actions or not, but we'll later learn (Day 34) that he has no expectation that they'll kill Jesus. Therefore, Judas may have assumed they'd arrest and detain him for a few days before releasing him. Or maybe he didn't consider Jesus at all, only focusing on his payout.

Though Matthew doesn't use the word *betray* in this passage, Mark and Luke do.

When it comes to Judas, I've heard the word *betray* so often that it's become commonplace and lost its meaning. The dictionary helps restore my understanding of the gravity of Judas's action.

At a basic level, *betray* means to be disloyal. Judas definitely does that. More specifically, *betray* means to violate a trust and deliver someone over to their enemy. Judas certainly does that too. On a national level, betray means to commit treason. It isn't much of a stretch to view Judas's betrayal of Jesus as an act of treason against God and his kingdom.

Interestingly, in Stephen's lengthy defense— effectively a sermon—before the Sanhedrin, he doesn't mention Judas as betraying Jesus. Instead, he accuses the religious leaders of betraying and murdering the Messiah (Acts 7:52).

Questions: *In what ways have we betrayed Jesus? If* betrayal *is too strong of a word, in what ways have we been disloyal to him?*

Prayer: Jesus, forgive us when we have been disloyal or betrayed you. Give us strength to not repeat those mistakes.

DAY 20, MONDAY: PASSOVER PREPARATIONS

TODAY'S PASSAGE: MATTHEW 26:17–19, MARK 14:12–16, AND LUKE 22:7–13

Focus verse: *"Go into the city to a certain man and tell him, 'The Teacher says: My appointed time is near. I am going to celebrate the Passover with my disciples at your house.'"* (Matthew 26:18)

The time for the Passover draws near. It's the reason Jesus and his disciples are in Jerusalem.

Passover is an annual celebration that began when the Israelites were slaves in Egypt. As instructed by Moses, each family slaughtered a lamb and roasted it over a fire. They feasted on the meat. They also took blood from the lamb and spread it on the doorframe of their house.

On the night of that first observance, God sent his angel to kill the firstborn of each house. But the angel would "pass over" the houses with blood on their doorposts (Exodus 12:1–30). This was the final plague, and at last the Pharaoh let the people leave Egypt. And when he later changed his mind and chased after them, God performed a miracle to wipe out the Egyptian army. This freed God's people from their masters and poised them to head toward the land God promised to give them.

The annual Passover celebration remembers all this. It's not a question of *if* Jesus and his disciples will observe the Passover, but *where*. When they ask what he has in mind, he gives a cryptic answer.

"Go to town and find a certain man. Tell him that the Teacher's appointed time draws near, and he and his disciples will celebrate Passover at his house." The disciples go and do as Jesus instructed. Though Matthew and Mark imply that all twelve disciples go, Luke says it's only Peter and John.

Though Matthew's account is concise, Mark and Luke give more detail. They both write that upon entering the city the disciples are to look for a man carrying a jar of water. They are to follow the man to his destination. Once they reach the house, they're to talk to the owner, who will take them to a large room, all furnished and ready. This is where they're to make the needed Passover preparations.

We understand that, culturally, women were the ones to fetch water, not men. So, a man carrying a water jug would stand out and be easy to spot. Though I've always assumed this takes place in Jerusalem, the Bible doesn't specify where. It's possible it happens in Bethany.

What's always amazed me is that the disciples' arrival and request doesn't surprise the owner of the house. Though we don't know if he realizes who the Teacher is, he has a large room ready for them to celebrate Passover.

I marvel over his faith to have made preparations before the disciples made their request and his ready acceptance of their presumptuous question of "Where is my guest room?"

Questions*: When has God told us to do something that made no sense? Did we have the faith to obey? How can we commemorate now what God has done for us in the past?*

Prayer: Jesus, when you tell us to do something, may we obey—even if we don't understand why.

DAY 21, TUESDAY: JESUS WASHES THE DISCIPLES' FEET

TODAY'S PASSAGE: JOHN 13:1–17

Focus verse: *Jesus answered, "Unless I wash you, you have no part with me."* (John 13:8)

With the Passover preparations complete, Jesus and the rest of the disciples arrive. Only John records what happens next. Though the owner of the house provided them with a large, furnished room to use, he didn't offer any of his staff to help.

Jesus and his disciples are there by themselves. This means there's no one to perform the customary foot washing. This isn't a polite ceremony but more of a physical necessity.

Most all the people travel by foot, including Jesus and his disciples. As they spend their day walking about, they stir up dust and sweat, making quite a mess on their feet. And, despite being careful, they no doubt step in feces from time to time. Even if they're fortunate enough to wear sandals, their feet would still be a disgusting mess by the end of the day.

The polite action of a host is to have someone wash their feet. We can expect this chore to go to the person of lowest stature. It would be a humbling and repulsive task. Surely, no one would volunteer to so debase themselves. This means the disciples will all have dirty feet tonight.

Yet Jesus, their leader, takes on this distasteful task.

One by one, he scrubs away the filth on his followers' feet. His action must mortify each one, seeing their Master, their Rabbi, degrade himself to do what no one else offered to do. We can suspect that each one wishes he'd done this and not let it fall to Jesus.

Peter, as is often the case, is the one to speak. He voices his unease, telling Jesus to not wash his feet.

Jesus tells Peter that he doesn't understand, but

later he will. "Unless I wash you," Jesus says, "you have no part with me."

Jesus must wash us.

Here he lowers himself to wash the disciples' feet. In a few days he will lower himself to die for all of us to wash away our sins. He will cleanse us. But if we don't accept him washing us clean, we can have no part in him.

Jesus says he did this as an example for the disciples to follow.

Does this mean we are to wash each other's feet in a literal sense?

Possibly. But the better lesson shows us the need to serve people in humility (see 1 Timothy 5:9–10). We should not expect others to serve us but seek ways to serve them. This applies even if we're a leader—maybe *especially* if we're a leader.

And washing feet is just one of many ways we can humble ourselves to serve people as Jesus commands us to do.

Questions: *How can we better serve others, regardless of how distasteful it may be? When have we expected others to serve us?*

Prayer: Jesus, may we seek to serve others just as you modeled for us.

DAY 22, WEDNESDAY: JESUS PREDICTS HIS BETRAYAL

TODAY'S PASSAGE: MATTHEW 26:20–25, MARK 14:17–21, LUKE 22:21–23, AND JOHN 13:18–30

Focus verse: *And while they were eating, he said, "Truly I tell you, one of you will betray me."* (Matthew 26:21)

Having washed his disciples' feet, Jesus now moves them into the Passover celebration. As they recline around the table, Jesus has some disheartening news to share first. "One of you will betray me."

This news saddens them. One by one they each say to him, "Surely you don't mean me?" Though eleven of the disciples ask this question sincerely, Judas can't. He knows it's him. Yet he joins them by giving his own false display of innocence. And Jesus indirectly confirms that it's Judas.

Some people give Judas a bit of acclaim for doing his part—however despicable—to bring about the events that lead to Jesus's sacrificial death on the cross to spare us from the death penalty that our sins deserve.

Yet it wasn't God's will for Judas to betray Jesus. Satan entered Judas (Luke 22:3 and John 13:27). Judas gave in to the temptation. But God used Judas's sin to bring about his divine plan. Though God worked out everything, he did so *despite* Judas, not *because of* him.

Jesus clearly states how he feels about his betrayer. "Woe to him. It would be better for him to have never been born." Judas is not a hero. He's not even an antihero. He is perhaps the most despicable of all people, having betrayed Jesus, the Son of God. It's hard to imagine a weightier sin.

John gives us more detail about this event, stirring in a bit of drama. After Jesus proclaims that one of his disciples will betray him, they're confused. Peter motions to John, who's next to Jesus, to find out what their leader means.

John tips his head toward Jesus and asks, "Who is it?"

Holding up a piece of bread, Jesus says, "it's the one I give this to." Then he dips the bread—

perhaps in olive oil or a sauce—and hands it to Judas (Psalm 41:9). It's confirmed.

"Now go do what you must do, and do it quickly."

But none of the disciples understand what happened. It's as if they have ears but cannot hear (see Jeremiah 5:21). Though Jesus's meaning is clear to us, it isn't to them. They explain away their confusion by assuming Jesus tells Judas to go buy something for the Passover celebration or give money to the poor.

The disciples hold to a fixed perspective of who Jesus is and specific expectations of what he'll do. Having Judas betray their Savior doesn't fit their assumptions, so they dismiss what Jesus says and try to twist it into something else that doesn't confront their point of view.

The same happens to many people today when they read the Bible. Though the message is clear, it doesn't fit their perspective of God or align with their expectations, so they dismiss what Scripture says and distort it to make it fit their own narrative.

They have ears but don't hear.

Questions*: What is our attitude toward Judas and what he did? When we read God's Word, how can we make sure we have ears that hear instead of trying to force Scripture to fit our limited perspective?*

Prayer: Lord, when you speak to us through your Word or Holy Spirit, may we have ears that hear what you're saying.

DAY 23, THURSDAY: THE LORD'S SUPPER

TODAY'S PASSAGE: MATTHEW 26:26–30, MARK 14:22–26, AND LUKE 22:14–20

Focus verse: *"Drink from it, all of you. This is my blood of the covenant, which is poured out for many for the forgiveness of sins."* (Matthew 26:27–28)

Having revealed the disconcerting news that one of Jesus's disciples will betray him, they continue with the Passover celebration. This festival is one of the Jews' more anticipated events of the year, perhaps the most. It's a high point in their annual calendar.

We've already covered the meaning behind Passover in Day 20. As we mentioned, Moses decreed it as an annual event to commemorate what God did when he rescued his people from their oppression.

Jesus and his disciples remember that day with their own Passover celebration. This is something Jesus wants to experience before the Roman soldiers execute him.

As they go through the Passover meal, Jesus adds a deeper meaning to their tradition. The bread they share symbolizes his body, which will soon be killed for them. The drink they share symbolizes his blood, which will soon flow from him as a new covenant poured out to forgive their sins, to wash their sins away (see Exodus 24:8 and Zechariah 9:11).

Depending on our tradition, we now call this new procedure Jesus implemented Holy Communion, the Eucharist, or the Lord's Supper.

Some followers of Jesus believe that the bread and wine taken during the celebration become the literal body and blood of Jesus. Others see the bread and wine as symbolic representations of the body and blood of Jesus.

Yet we need not debate this. What matters is that we partake to remember Jesus. That's the point.

But how we partake today bears little resemblance to the practice Jesus implemented two thousand years ago.

Passover is an annual event. It occurs at home with family and friends. And it's part of a meal—a feast. Jesus doesn't change any of these basic elements when he adds our Communion practices to Passover.

When we partake today in our Sunday church service, we lose sight of all three factors. It's not annual, it's not at home, and it's not in a family setting. Drinking a sip of juice and nibbling on a cracker pales in the light of the significant celebration that Jesus instituted so that we'd remember him and what he did for us.

I'm not suggesting we should forgo the rite of the Eucharist in a church service. But I advocate that we work to reclaim the Lord's Supper as the celebration Jesus implemented and intended for us to follow.

Questions*: What can we do to give more meaning to our practice of the Lord's Supper? How can we better commemorate what Jesus did and who he is?*

Prayer: Jesus, may we never partake of your Holy Supper again without fully celebrating who you are and what you did to save us. Thank you, Jesus.

DAY 24, FRIDAY: JESUS PREDICTS PETER'S DENIAL

TODAY'S PASSAGE: MATTHEW 26:31–35, MARK 14:27–31, LUKE 22:31–34, AND JOHN 13:36–38

Focus verse: *"Truly I tell you," Jesus answered, "this very night, before the rooster crows, you will disown me three times."* (Matthew 26:34)

Jesus and his disciples have completed their Passover celebration. Since Judas left during the meal to betray Jesus, only eleven disciples remain. I expect they're still basking in the celebration's aftermath. Yet Judas's absence looms as a reminder of Jesus's confusing words about his betrayal.

As they leave the house where they celebrated Passover, Jesus has more to tell his remaining followers. "You will all desert me, just as the prophet predicted: 'I will strike the shepherd and the sheep will scatter'" (Zechariah 13:7).

Peter, no doubt with Jesus's prediction of betrayal on his mind, is quick to assert his loyalty. "Even if everyone else deserts you, I never will."

"I tell you the truth," Jesus said, "even tonight, before dawn breaks, you will disown me three times."

"Even if I must die," Peter answers, "I will never disown you."

All the other disciples say the same thing.

I'm sure Peter means what he says. I'm sure the other ten disciples do too. Yet, despite their pledge of loyalty, it won't be long before they all sprint away in fear.

And despite Peter's adamant declaration of his willingness to die for Jesus, we'll soon see that he disavows Jesus three times over the next few hours. In short, he will fail to acknowledge any affiliation with the Messiah (see Day 33).

Like Judas (see Day 19), Peter will, in his own way, betray Jesus. Though there's a difference between Judas's betrayal and Peter's denial, failing to acknowledge his association with Jesus is a small, but real, act of betrayal.

Besides the severity of their respective disloyalties, Luke explains another difference. In his passage covering this event, Jesus says, "I prayed for you, Simon Peter, that your faith will stay strong. And after you come back, strengthen your brothers."

How encouraging to know that Jesus prayed for Peter to remain strong in the face of the three temptations he'll encounter to deny any affiliation with Jesus. Yet Jesus knows Peter will still falter, so the Lord tacks on a second part to his prayer. He prays that Peter—after he repents of his sins—will take the lead in strengthening the other ten disciples of Jesus.

And this is precisely what happens.

Questions: *In what ways have we not acknowledged Jesus or denied we're one of his followers? Though it's a loaded word, how have we betrayed Jesus?*

Prayer: Jesus, may we never deny or betray you. And if we do, may you quickly restore us into right relationship with you.

DAY 25, SATURDAY: TWO SWORDS

TODAY'S PASSAGE: LUKE 22:35–38

Focus verse: *"If you don't have a sword, sell your cloak and buy one."* (Luke 22:36)

As Jesus and his disciples continue their journey to where they'll spend the night, Jesus has another teaching for them. Luke records the scene for us.

Jesus has them recall the time when he sent them out, two by two, to heal people and preach a message of repentance (Mark 6:7–13). He had told them to take nothing with them for their journey and now asks them to reflect on what they lacked.

"Nothing," they say.

Even so, he gives them new instructions. He tells

them to take a purse (implying money) and a bag (implying provisions). "And if you don't have a sword, sell your cloak to buy one." Then he quotes the prophet Isaiah, about the Savior being numbered with the transgressors (Isaiah 53:12).

"We have two swords," the disciples say.

Did you catch that? Jesus's disciples carry swords.

I've never envisioned Jesus's band of followers as brandishing weapons. I've seen several paintings, along with many more movies, but never once do I remember a disciple with a sword strapped to his waist. The thought shocks me, yet when Jesus tells them to buy a sword, they already have two.

If I were picking people to start a spiritual movement, I'd certainly rule out anyone who carried a weapon. Yet, Jesus has different criteria. He accepts his followers as they are. They have issues, baggage, problems . . . and swords.

Now, back to our story. Upon hearing that they have two swords, Jesus replies, "That's enough!"

Jesus's response is perplexing. What does he mean?

Though the immediate assumption is that they'll need the swords that very night, this misses Jesus's intent, as we'll soon see when he tells them to put their swords away. Another consideration is that carrying two swords is enough to "number them with the transgressors" according to the Old Testament prophecy he just quoted.

Yet we can also read this as one of exasperation. Jesus tried to instruct them, and they missed his point. By saying "That's enough!" he says to stop talking about it.

We'll later read that when Jesus prays for his disciples (Day 28), he'll confirm that while he was with them, he protected them and kept them safe (John 17:12). So it was when he sent them on their journey. But once he leaves this earth, he'll no longer be present to protect them. Therefore, they'll need to take reasonable precautions and avoid unnecessary risks as they continue without him.

This means that, once Jesus is gone, they'll need to travel with purse, bag, and sword. But since he is still with them, the swords aren't necessary.

As we read the rest of the New Testament, we see no mention of his followers carrying swords. Yet Paul hints at this when he tells the church in Ephesus to put on the sword of the Spirit, that is, the word of God. This is the only offensive weapon in the armor of God (Ephesians 6:10–17).

Though most people assume the sword of the

Spirit is the *written* word of God, the New Testament didn't exist when Paul wrote his letter. A better understanding is that Paul refers to the *spoken* word of God, that is, the words of the Holy Spirit.

Might Jesus be telling his disciples they'll need the Holy Spirit—the sword of the Spirit—to protect them when he's gone?

Questions: *How should we react when we can interpret a passage of Scripture in multiple ways? What role does the Holy Spirit play in our lives today?*

Prayer: Heavenly Father, grant us peace when we don't understand a passage of the Bible. Holy Spirit, give us insight for those times when our own understanding isn't enough.

DAY 26, SUNDAY: JESUS PRAYS AT THE GARDEN OF GETHSEMANE

TODAY'S PASSAGE: MATTHEW 26:36–46, MARK 14:32–44, AND LUKE 22:39–46

Focus verse: *"My Father, if it is possible, may this cup be taken from me. Yet not as I will, but as you will."* (Matthew 26:39)

Having confronted Peter about denying him and talking about swords, Jesus and his disciples continue walking. They reach the Garden of Gethsemane. Nonbiblical sources say that Gethsemane is at the base of the Mount of Olives, where Jesus and his disciples often withdraw to.

He tells them to sit while he prays. Taking Peter, James, and John with him, sorrow overwhelms his soul over what awaits him. "Stay here," Jesus says, "and keep watch with me."

He goes further away—Luke says a stone's throw. Jesus falls to the ground and prays. "Father, if possible, take this cup from me, but not my will but yours."

In praying this, Jesus may recall the story of Abraham and Isaac in the Old Testament. Isaac is the only son of Abraham and Sarah. From Isaac will come Abraham's legacy, fulfilling God's promise to make him into the father of many nations.

Yet despite this, God tells Abraham to sacrifice his son—his only son—to him. Abraham intends to obey. With Isaac bound and lying on the altar, Abraham raises his knife to slay his son. At the last moment, God stops Abraham. God has a plan B and supplies a ram to die instead of Isaac (Genesis 22:1–19 and Hebrews 11:17–19).

This is only a test of Abraham's loyalty to God and of his obedience—in the most extreme situation. Abraham passes God's test, and Isaac lives.

When Jesus asks his Father to take this cup away from him, is he recalling this story about Abraham and how it was a test of obedience? Just as Abraham didn't have to sacrifice his only son, perhaps Jesus hopes his Father won't follow through and sacrifice *his* only Son.

This may be what Jesus is praying for, but, more importantly, he is willing to submit to his Father's will.

After completing his prayer, Jesus returns to his disciples and finds them asleep. They failed to watch with him, even for an hour. Though Jesus prayed for an hour, Matthew, Mark, and Luke only record two sentences from his prayer. They must think these are the two most important lines.

Jesus repeats his request to his disciples, reminding them that the spirit is willing, but the flesh is weak. He prays the same prayer a second time.

When he returns, he finds them sleeping again. This repeats a third time. By now the opportunity for prayer has passed. Judas is about to betray Jesus so the religious leaders can arrest him. There is no plan B, and Jesus submits to his Father's will.

Though God spared Abraham's son from a sacrificial death, he didn't spare his own son from dying for us.

Questions: *How can we support others by keeping watch with them? How can we cause our spirit to triumph over our flesh? Are we willing to obey Father God regardless of the cost?*

Prayer: Lord, may we always obey you, regardless of the circumstances. May we do your will in all situations.

DAY 27, MONDAY: JESUS PRAYS FOR HIMSELF

TODAY'S PASSAGE: JOHN 17:1–5

Focus verse: *"Father, the hour has come. Glorify your Son, that your Son may glorify you."* (John 17:1)

While Matthew, Mark, and Luke give us a short two-sentence summary of Jesus's hour-long prayer, John gives us much more detail. We find this recorded in John 17.

It's Jesus's longest prayer in the Bible. It's also the most momentous. Jesus, knowing that his execution is imminent, can spend his last hours on earth in a variety of ways. Yet he prays. We should pay attention to what he says.

To consider this long prayer, we'll divide it into

three sections. In the opening, Jesus prays for himself and glory for both him and the Father. In the second part, he prays for his disciples. And for the third part, he prays for us.

In the first segment of this prayer, with Jesus praying for himself, the words *glorify* and *glory* occur several times. Jesus opens with a request that God will glorify him. Though we may think in terms of glorifying God (1 Corinthians 10:31 and Ephesians 1:11–12), Jesus turns it around, asking God to glorify him. If not for the fact that he's the Son of God, this would seem presumptuous.

How will Father God glorify Jesus?

By sustaining him through his ordeal unto death, by accepting his sacrifice for our sins, and by raising him from the dead. In doing so, Jesus's obedience to God's plan will bring glory to his Father. It's a mutual exchange of giving glory to each other. Yet we realize that Jesus and his Father are one (John 17:11, 21–22). It's a heady realization and challenging to understand, but with the Father and Son giving glory to each other, God effectively gives glory to himself.

The result of this glory is to offer us eternal life.

As he prays, Jesus defines eternal life as knowing the Father and knowing Jesus the Messiah, sent by the Father. If we know Jesus, we know the Father, and are in intimate relationship with them. This eternal life connection starts now, and it continues throughout our life and into the afterlife. Knowing Jesus and the one true God positions us to live with them forever. This is eternal life.

Though Jesus has not yet died, at this point in his prayer he foresees the successful completion of his mission. This brings glory to the Father. And Jesus will return to his Father's presence and receive glory, as it has always been, even before our world's creation.

Questions: *How can we give glory to God? Might God ever decide to give glory to us? What is our response to this thought?*

Prayer: Heavenly Father, may we live lives that glorify you. Show us how to best do this.

DAY 28, TUESDAY: JESUS PRAYS FOR HIS DISCIPLES

TODAY'S PASSAGE: JOHN 17:6–19

Focus verse: *"Holy Father, protect them by the power of your name, the name you gave me, so that they may be one as we are one."* (John 17:11)

The second segment of Jesus's prayer focuses on his disciples. He has spent three years with them, teaching them all that they need to know to continue his mission and further advance the Kingdom of God once he returns to heaven.

If they falter in this, the world will never hear about Jesus. As a result, only a small segment might receive his redeeming grace and mercy. The disciples must persevere if Jesus's church is to grow.

There is much packed into this brief passage. This includes that Jesus receives glory through them, that Jesus wants them to experience his full joy, and that the world hates them. We also see that Judas is doomed to destruction for his betrayal of Jesus—even though God used it to carry out his purpose.

Each of these items calls for further consideration.

Three other things, however, stand out in Jesus's prayer for his disciples. He makes three significant requests to Papa.

Unify: The first petition is to unify them. Jesus tells us he and his Father are one. In the same way he wants his disciples to be one, to get along. He prays for their unity.

Why is this important? If they can't get along with each other, their division will hamper their witness to the world, which needs to hear about Jesus.

As we read the book of Acts, we see a lot of unity in the early church. And for those times when conflict arose, the leaders of Jesus's church handle the discord quickly and conclusively.

We can learn from their example today. We *must*

learn from it if we hope to be effective in reaching the world for Jesus.

Protect: The second request Jesus makes for his disciples is to protect them. This first occurs when Jesus prays for their unity. "Protect them so they may be one," Jesus says. Though he protected them and kept them safe while he was with them, when he goes away, he won't be able to do that. He'll leave this world, and they'll stay.

Notice that he doesn't ask Father God to remove them from the world, but to protect them while they are in it and from the evil one. We might wish God would whisk us from this world and its many troubles as soon as we follow Jesus. But if he did that there'd be no one left to tell those who remain about him.

Sanctify: The third significant appeal Jesus makes for his disciples is that God will sanctify them. To sanctify means to set them apart as holy and make them right. This process of sanctification began when they first followed Jesus. It will continue to unfold throughout the rest of their lives as they become more like him.

Their sanctification will draw them closer to God and make their witness for Jesus more effective. Jesus wants the people they meet to see they are distinctive and offer a compelling difference from the world's ways.

Questions: *How does Jesus's prayer for his disciples' unity relate to us today? How are we doing on our journey of ongoing sanctification?*

Prayer: Jesus, may our unity with your children serve as an act of worship to the Father and an effective witness to our world.

DAY 29, WEDNESDAY: JESUS PRAYS FOR US

TODAY'S PASSAGE: JOHN 17:20–26

Focus verse: *"I have given them the glory that you gave me, that they may be one as we are one—I in them and you in me—so that they may be brought to complete unity."*
(John 17:22–23)

Having prayed for himself and for his disciples, Jesus wraps up his lengthy appeal to his Father by praying for all those who will one day believe in his disciples' message. This is a forward-thinking request that refers to you and me now. Yes, two thousand years ago Jesus prayed for us who live today. We should take his prayer most seriously.

In this section of his prayer, we see the recurring

theme of glory, which appeared in the first two segments, smartly connecting all three. We also see Jesus again mentioning that he and his Father are one. As Jesus desires his disciples to be one with him and Papa, he also wants us today—all who believe in his message—to be one with them.

As the Father and Son unite to function as one, so too should we unite as one with them, to be of one mind and one spirit. The indirect result of this unity is harmony and peace. But the direct, stated purpose of our unity is so that the world will know Jesus, sent by Father God out of his immense love to save them.

Yet when we don't get along with each other, we hamper our effectiveness of sharing God's love with them and the good news of Jesus the Christ to save them. When the Church of Jesus forms factions and bickers with each other, we tarnish our reputation and diminish our chances to tell others about our Savior.

Are our squabbles about doctrine, faith practices, and religious preferences more important than the impact of our message, which is perfected when we get along? Each time a new Protestant denomination forms, each time a church splits, and each time one minister attacks another, they act against

Jesus's prayer that we will be one. And each time we, as individuals, align with one of those divisions, we do our part to thwart the unity Jesus prayed for us to have.

When Christians don't get along with other Christians, no one wins—and the world loses. This is completely unacceptable; it's incompatible with Jesus's prayer that we'll be one and live in unity.

Questions: *How well do we practice unity today? How well does our church pursue unity? What can we do to change this?*

Prayer: Lord, strengthen us to be one, just as you —Father and Son—are one, so that the world may know you.

DAY 30, THURSDAY: JESUS ARRESTED

TODAY'S PASSAGE: MATTHEW 26:47–56, MARK
14:43–52, LUKE 22:47–53, AND JOHN 18:1–12

Focus verse: *Now the betrayer had arranged a signal
with them: "The one I kiss is the man; arrest him."*
(Matthew 26:48)

With Jesus having prayed, Judas arrives with the mob to arrest him.

Judas walks up to Jesus and greets him with a kiss. This signals the mob who to arrest. How it must pain Jesus for Judas to give him this false display of affection. Judas may have picked this signal because it was an action he'd done in the past and would seem natural. Yet why the pretense? It will soon be clear that Judas has betrayed his master, so why attempt to camouflage his treachery with a kiss?

Matthew, Mark, and Luke all mention the treacherous kiss, yet John doesn't. Instead, in John's account, Jesus asks the mob, led by Judas, "Who do you want?"

"Jesus of Nazareth," they answer.

"I am he." By saying this, he implies he is God. "I AM" is how God identified himself to Moses (Exodus 3:14).

At this, the people pull back and fall to the ground. This could be because they bow in reverence to God. Or, not accepting that Jesus is God, it could be they pull back in fear that the Almighty will strike Jesus dead for claiming to be God.

A disciple—John says it's Peter—pulls out his sword and cuts off the ear of the high priest's servant. Peter is a fisherman and not a soldier. He's not skilled using a weapon. We don't know if he makes a forward thrust at the chest, a sideways swing to the neck, or a downward blow on the head, but he misses his mark and all he gets is an ear.

After telling Peter to put away his sword, a delightful detail in Luke's account is that Jesus heals the man's wound. Even in the middle of his arrest and imminent execution, Jesus still cares for the needs of others.

Jesus turns to address the crowd.

He asks why they traveled at night to arrest him, when they could have easily done so during the day at the temple. This confirms that Jesus knows the religious leaders worry about the people's reaction should they arrest him in public. That's why they chose a remote location and at night with few people around (Luke 22:6).

After this, the disciples scatter and desert Jesus, leaving him alone. Yet he still has his Father in heaven with him—for now.

Questions: *Which aspect of Jesus's arrest most affects you? Which part most perplexes you?*

Prayer: Holy Spirit, teach us and reveal truth to us through the actions of Judas, Peter, and the rest of the disciples.

DAY 31, FRIDAY: THE RELIGIOUS LEADERS INTERROGATE JESUS

TODAY'S PASSAGE: MATTHEW 26:57–63, MARK 14:53–61, AND JOHN 18:12–14, 19–24

Focus verse: *The chief priests and the whole Sanhedrin were looking for false evidence against Jesus so that they could put him to death.* (Matthew 26:59)

After the mob arrests Jesus, they haul him back to Jerusalem. There Jesus stands trial before the religious leaders. The four accounts of this event (we'll look at Luke's on Day 32) use varying labels, but they all encompass the religious leaders. These include the high priest Caiaphas, Annas (Caiaphas's father-in-law), the chief priests, the teachers of the law, and the whole Sanhedrin, also known as the Council.

Caiaphas told the religious leaders that it

would be good for one man to die for all the people (John 11:49–51). And now he's present, leading the initiative to do just that. Did he plan this all along?

We see these people and groups band together for a concerted push to convict Jesus of something —anything—so they can concoct a justification for killing him. It's collusion. And when collusion occurs under the cover of religion, it's the most despicable kind.

Lacking facts, they seek false evidence so they can charge him. This proceeding not only has a predetermined outcome, but we can suspect it's also an illegal gathering, one hastily convened in the middle of the night. They want to carry out their unjust actions before dawn, so the masses can't see what they're doing and oppose it.

The religious leaders call many false witnesses, but these scoundrels contradict each other and fail to supply the damning evidence the council seeks. Given that these proceedings take place in the middle of the night, coherent testimony is likely hard to find, with only those carousing in the darkness available to testify.

At last, they find two false witnesses who will corroborate each other's story. They testify that they heard Jesus say he could destroy the temple of God and rebuild it in three days.

Though this is partly true—and may be what they thought they heard—it isn't what Jesus said. What he said was "Destroy this temple, and I will raise it again in three days" (John 2:18–21). He wasn't talking about the physical temple. Instead, he meant the temple of his body, which would miraculously rise from the dead three days after his detractors kill him.

At last, two witnesses agree. Although what they claim he said seems impossible and may offend the religious leaders, it hardly calls for the death penalty. Yet two agreeing witnesses is what the Old Testament law specifies as the minimum requirement to convict someone (Deuteronomy 19:15).

Throughout all this, Jesus says nothing.

Questions: *Why do you think Jesus remained quiet? When we see others banding together to do what is wrong, how can we oppose them and pursue justice?*

Prayer: Lord, show us how to do what is right even when it's hard.

DAY 32, SATURDAY: JESUS SUPPLIES THE TESTIMONY THEY SEEK

TODAY'S PASSAGE: MATTHEW 26:63–68, MARK 14:61–65, AND LUKE 22:66–71

Focus verse: *Then the high priest tore his clothes and said, "He has spoken blasphemy! Why do we need any more witnesses?"* (Matthew 26:65)

Throughout these unjust proceedings, Jesus doesn't defend himself. Even the two witnesses who misquote him aren't enough to rouse him to say anything. Though can give his version of what he said—and seek to correct the record—he doesn't.

This aligns with the prophetic words given by Isaiah several centuries earlier. The prophet wrote that he (the Messiah), though oppressed and afflicted, didn't say a thing. He remained silent (Isaiah 53:7).

Jesus, however, may not see a need to defend himself. All that would do is hold up the proceedings and delay the reason he came to earth in the first place: to die for us. Why would he want to forestall his mission and what was going to happen anyway?

In aggravation, the high priest, Caiaphas, addresses Jesus directly. Charging him under oath of the living God, Caiaphas implores Jesus, "Tell us if you are the Messiah, the Son of God."

At last Jesus speaks. It may be he wants to move things toward their predetermined end. Or the instruction to respond under oath by the living God may compel Jesus to answer.

In Matthew's account, Jesus opens with "You have said so."

Yet Mark shares the simpler and more damning statement of Jesus responding to Caiaphas's question by saying "I am." Those present would clearly see this as Jesus placing himself on the same level as God, who self-identifies as "I AM" (Exodus 3:14).

Jesus continues his reply. "In addition, let me say that from now on you'll see the Son of Man sitting on the right hand of God—the Mighty One —and coming on the clouds of heaven."

At this, Caiaphas tears his clothes in a physical display of outrage. "Blasphemy!" he cries out. "Blasphemy! Why do we need any more witnesses? What do you say?"

"He deserves death," the religious leaders reply.

They spit in Jesus's face and hit him with their fists. They slap and mock him.

Though the religious leaders failed to build a sufficient case against Jesus, he gave them all the testimony they needed. By claiming to be equal to God, they feel justified in condemning Jesus to die.

Questions: *Should we follow Jesus's example and say nothing when we're misquoted or wrongly accused? What does the word* blasphemy *mean to you?*

Prayer: Holy Spirit, when we're attacked or treated wrongly, give us clarity on how to respond and, if needed, the words to say.

DAY 33, SUNDAY: PETER DISOWNS JESUS

TODAY'S PASSAGE: MATTHEW 26:69–75, MARK 14:66–72, LUKE 22:54–62, AND JOHN 18:15–18, 25–27

Focus verse: *He denied it again, with an oath: "I don't know the man!"* (Matthew 26:72)

Of all Jesus's disciples, we know the most about Peter. On a personal level, he was married and might be the oldest of the group. We get a hint of this when the collectors of the temple tax ask Jesus why he hasn't paid. Jesus supplies a means to cover his and Peter's tax but not the other disciples (Matthew 17:24–27). This suggests they weren't old enough to need to pay the tax, while Peter was.

Peter, along with brothers James and John, is part of Jesus's inner circle. The three were there at

Jesus's transfiguration (Day 2) and his prayer in the Garden of Gethsemane (Day 26).

Of the disciples, Peter often speaks first, while the others remain quiet. As such he emerges as the spokesman of the twelve.

Though often criticized for a lack of faith during his short stint of walking on water, only Peter dares to climb out of the boat. It is confident Peter who pledges his loyalty to Jesus, willing to go to prison and even die for his master. And bold Peter pulls out his sword to defend Jesus.

These glimpses into Peter help us better understand him.

After Jesus's arrest, the disciples scatter, including Peter. If they stick around, they risk being rounded up too. Though the mob can't seize them all, they might be able to grab one or two more. And Peter—who assaulted and wounded another man—is a prime choice. Had he not run, the mob might have captured Peter along with Jesus. Fleeing was the safe decision.

Yet as Judas and the mob leave with Jesus, Peter follows at a distance (Matthew 26:58, Mark 14:54, and Luke 22:54). This may be because of his pledge to go to jail or even die for Jesus. Though running away in fear was an impulse, he now gathers his courage and trails behind the throng, hoping for a chance to make amends or looking for a way to save Jesus.

During the proceedings, Peter sits in the courtyard of the high priest Caiaphas's house. A servant recognizes him as one of Jesus's disciples, but Peter denies it, saying he has no idea what she's talking about.

Another servant confirms what the first one said. Peter again denies it. This time he says he doesn't even know the man—despite having spent the last three years with him.

Later a third person says, "Surely, you're one of them. Your accent gives you away." Peter denies any affiliation with Jesus a third time. He calls down curses on himself if he's lying and swears, "I don't know the man!"

At that moment, the rooster crows. This jogs Peter's memory of Jesus's prediction that before the rooster crows at dawn, Peter would have denied him three times.

Luke adds an interesting detail, noting that, when the rooster crows, Jesus turns and looks right at Peter. This shows us how near Peter is to Jesus.

John adds that the third person to question Peter is a relative of the man whose ear the disciple cut off. This person was also part of the mob sent to arrest Jesus. He's an eyewitness that Peter was with Jesus and committed an act of violence.

Peter leaves and cries bitter tears of remorse.

Questions: *How do we react when we sin, do something we promised not to do, or make a serious mistake? Do we run away from conflict? How do we know when we should fight or flee?*

Prayer: Father, give us strength to do what we promised and the ability to make the right choices in adverse situations.

DAY 34, MONDAY: JUDAS HANGS HIMSELF

TODAY'S PASSAGE: MATTHEW 27:1–10

Focus verse: *"I have sinned," [Judas] said, "for I have betrayed innocent blood."* (Matthew 27:4)

Though Scripture tells us much about Peter, it doesn't say much at all about Judas, also known as Judas Iscariot. We best know Judas for his betrayal of Jesus. Some passages in the Bible call him a traitor. That's a more fitting label, a traitor to Jesus.

Judas agrees to inform on Jesus and help the religious authorities arrest him. He does this for thirty pieces of silver. Money matters more to him than loyalty. We discussed some of his possible motivations in Day 19.

Judas also serves as the group's treasurer. He is dishonest, skimming funds from the community purse for personal use. Though he sometimes pretends to care about the needs of the poor, he doesn't. He's selfish, and each time they give money to those in need, the balance in their fund drops, making it harder for Judas to steal from what's left.

When Jesus eats the Passover meal with his disciples, he says that one of them will betray him. When they ask who, Jesus says it's the one he'll give the bread to. He dips the bread and hands it to Judas, telling him to "go do it quickly." The disciples miss his meaning and assume he's telling Judas to give money to the poor. Instead, Judas leaves so he can lead the mob to arrest Jesus (see Day 22).

The last time Mark, Luke, and John mention Judas is when he betrays Jesus with a kiss. It's as if after his despicable act he deserves no more coverage in Jesus's story. Matthew, however, tells us what happens next.

When Judas realizes the religious leaders have condemned Jesus to die, remorse overwhelms him. His selfish act to earn some easy money—thirty pieces of silver—set in motion the sham of a trial that found Jesus guilty of blasphemy and worthy of death.

This ruling surprises Judas. It wasn't what he expected. It's not the outcome he wanted. Overcome with guilt, he tries to return the thirty pieces of silver. "I've betrayed an innocent man," he says. This can't undo his grave mistake, but it is a slight gesture to show his repentance.

The religious leaders don't care and won't accept the repayment. They call it blood money, even though they were the ones to give it to Judas in the first place, revealing their hypocrisy and double standard.

Since they won't take the money back, Judas throws the thirty coins into the temple and leaves. The words of Jesus may echo in his ears: "Woe to the man who betrays me. It would be better if he had never been born."

Judas leaves and kills himself.

Questions: *Is any sin so big that Jesus can't forgive it? What other options did Judas have?*

Prayer: Jesus, when we make a grave mistake, may we not give up. Instead may we seek you in remorse and repent.

DAY 35, TUESDAY: JESUS COMES BEFORE PILATE

TODAY'S PASSAGE: MATTHEW 27:11–14, MARK 15:1–5, LUKE 23:1–9, AND JOHN 18:28–38

Focus verse: *[Pilate] asked him, "Are you the king of the Jews?" "You have said so," Jesus replied.* (Matthew 27:11)

A lthough the Roman overseers allow the religious leaders some degree of self-rule, they may not execute anyone. Only Rome can do that. So, after decreeing that Jesus must die for blasphemy, the religious leaders drag him to Pilate, the Roman governor of the area.

The Bible tells us only two other things about Pilate. First, we learn that Pilate is governor of Judea (and Herod is tetrarch of Galilee) when John the Baptist starts his ministry (Luke 3:1).

The other mention of Pilate is a vague reference to a barbarous act when he mixed the blood of some Galileans in with their sacrifices (Luke 13:1). Scripture doesn't tell us what these people did or why Pilate responded the way he did, but it's easy to view him as a man who cares little about the Jewish people he oversees.

The third and final time we read about Pilate in the Gospels is when Jesus comes before him.

Matthew's account of this event is the most concise of all four: Jesus stands before the governor. Pilate asks him if he's the king of the Jews. Jesus says he is. The Jewish leaders throw accusations at him, but he doesn't respond, much to Pilate's amazement.

Luke notes that they also accuse him of misleading the people and opposing Roman taxation.

In contrast, John gives us the most detail about Jesus as he stands before Pilate.

It's early morning when they arrive at Pilate's palace. Since Pilate is a Gentile, they'll defile themselves if they go inside.

Pilate comes out. "What are the charges?"

They dodge his question. "If he weren't guilty, we wouldn't have brought him to you."

"Deal with the issue yourself, according to your own law," Pilate says.

"But we can't execute anyone," they respond.

Pilate goes inside and questions Jesus. "Are you the king of the Jews?"

They banter a bit about Jesus being a king. Then Jesus adds that his kingdom is not of this world and the reason he was born was to testify to the truth. "Everyone who cares about truth listens to me."

"What is truth?" Pilate asks rhetorically.

Then he returns to tell the religious leaders that he found no justification to execute their king.

Luke adds a detail to our story that the other writers omit. When he learns Jesus is a Galilean, Pilate sends Jesus to Herod, the tetrarch of Galilee.

Questions: *What is the truth Jesus testifies about? How do you understand Jesus's kingdom?*

Prayer: Jesus, may we discern what is true and advance your kingdom.

DAY 36, WEDNESDAY: JESUS COMES BEFORE HEROD

TODAY'S PASSAGE: LUKE 23:7–12

Focus verse: *[Herod] plied him with many questions, but Jesus gave him no answer.* (Luke 23:9)

Two men named Herod are part of Jesus's story. The first Herod (history calls him Herod the Great) tries to kill Jesus shortly after he's born. To escape his reach, Jesus's parents take their baby to Egypt. When Herod dies, they return.

The second Herod is the son of the first, ruling over one fourth of his father's realm (a tetrarch). He is the Herod referred to in today's passage.

Scripture tells us a bit about this Herod. Three

stories reveal his character, or, more precisely, his lack of character.

First, he marries Herodias after he takes her from her first husband—his own brother. John the Baptizer criticizes their marriage, and Herod throws him in prison. In this we see Herod punishing an innocent man in an act of personal retaliation.

Next, Herodias uses a situation with her daughter to manipulate Herod into killing John. Though Herod could and should have said no, he gives in to Herodias's manipulation and orders John's execution by beheading. In doing so, Herod kills a man to avoid a public embarrassment.

Now we see Herod when the religious leaders condemn Jesus to die for blasphemy. They first bring Jesus to Pilate, who sends him to Herod because Herod oversees Galilee and Jesus is from there. The case falls under Herod's rule, and Herod is in Jerusalem at the time.

This pleases Herod, not because he wants to rule on Jesus's situation but because he's wanted for a long time to see Jesus, hoping to witness a miracle. Herod asks Jesus question after question, but Jesus doesn't answer a single one. All this time the religious leaders throw accusation after accusation at Jesus.

Herod interrogates him. The religious leaders accuse him. And Jesus says nothing, just as Isaiah prophesied (Isaiah 53:7).

Getting nowhere with his questions, and with little chance of seeing a miracle, Herod mocks Jesus. So do his soldiers. They put an elegant robe on him—not out of reverence but ridicule.

After tiring of their sport, Herod sends Jesus back to Pilate. Herod didn't need to do that. He could have kept Jesus under his jurisdiction and saved him from death. Instead, Herod takes the simple way out.

In doing so, he plays a part in Jesus's death.

Questions: *When have we done what was easy instead of what was right? When have we been quiet when other people mocked Jesus?*

Prayer: Lord, strengthen us to do what is right instead of what is easy.

DAY 37, THURSDAY: BARABBAS

TODAY'S PASSAGE: MATTHEW 27:15–26, MARK 15:6–11, LUKE 23:18–19, AND JOHN 18:39–40

Focus verse: *Pilate asked them, "Which one do you want me to release to you: Jesus Barabbas, or Jesus who is called the Messiah?"* (Matthew 27:17)

With Herod sending Jesus back to Pilate, the scene reverts to the governor's palace. He may have thought that by sending Jesus to Herod he had passed the situation on to someone else and avoided further involvement. But Herod passes things back to Pilate. This means Pilate has no choice but to deal with Jesus.

Pilate established a practice of releasing a prisoner each year at Passover. This was a strategic move to garner some goodwill from the Jews who hate him, along with the Roman rule he represents. Since he picked Passover, he can do this when Jerusalem overflows with people. This maximizes the impact of his generosity. He even lets the people pick who he releases. We can expect the masses to request the release of someone wrongly imprisoned.

Knowing the religious leaders' motivation for wanting to kill Jesus and thinking he has a clever way out of the situation, Pilate decides to ask the people who they want him to release this year. He expects them to say Jesus.

But when Pilate asks his customary question, the mob shouts their request. "Barabbas!"

Since he only appears in this one scene, Scripture tells us little about Barabbas. All we know is that he's in prison for insurrection and murder. He's certainly not someone wrongly imprisoned. Because he's held on murder charges, he may face crucifixion. He probably sits on their version of death row awaiting his execution, perhaps even as soon as the Passover celebration ends.

Though the people requesting he release Barabbas surprises Pilate, it's what the religious leaders orchestrated by stirring up the crowd to ask for the notorious Barabbas instead of Jesus.

They don't want Jesus freed—the one who came to heal and save them. Instead, they want a murderer released back into society. This makes no sense, but mobs never do.

Unable to dissuade them, and wanting to avoid a riot, Pilate releases Barabbas. Barabbas, who deserves death, is set free, and Jesus, who is without fault, will die instead.

The Bible tells us nothing more about Barabbas. We're left to wonder how he reacts to the second chance Jesus gives him by dying in his place.

Questions: *How do we react to Jesus dying in our place? What are we doing with the second chance Jesus gives us when we follow him?*

Prayer: Thank you, Jesus, for dying for us so that we can live with you forever.

DAY 38, FRIDAY: PILATE'S DECISION

TODAY'S PASSAGE: MATTHEW 27:19, 24–26,
MARK 15:12–15, LUKE 23:13–17, 20–25, AND
JOHN 19:6–16

Focus verse: *[Herod] released Barabbas to them. But he had Jesus flogged, and handed him over to be crucified.*
(Matthew 27:26)

Throughout the biblical narrative we see that Pilate wants to release Jesus and tries to do so—multiple times. He knows Jesus is innocent and is only there because of the religious leaders' jealousy.

Surely Pilate realizes the religious leaders stirred up the people to request the release of Barabbas instead of Jesus. Since they paid Judas to betray Jesus, is there any reason to think they wouldn't also pay some ringleaders to rile up the crowd to demand Jesus's death?

Matthew also records three interesting reveals that the other biographers of Jesus skip.

The first is that, in the middle of the proceedings, Pilate receives an urgent message from his wife. She affirms Jesus's innocence and urges her husband to have nothing to do with him. Why does she say this? Because she had a dream about Jesus and suffered much through it.

Yet it's too late for Pilate to not get involved. He already is. He wants to release Jesus, but the crowd won't accept it. They demand his crucifixion. Pilate is about to have a riot on his hands—a scenario he must avoid, lest his superiors hold him accountable for it.

The second item Matthew mentions is that when Pilate realizes he won't be able to release Jesus without causing a riot, he washes his hands in a bowl of water. He does this in front of the crowd. In doing so, he symbolically shows he wants no part in Jesus's death and proclaims he's innocent of what the people clamor for. "You are responsible," he concludes.

Yet Pilate isn't innocent. For Jesus to die by

crucifixion, Pilate must approve it. By allowing it to occur, he's likewise guilty.

The people's response is the third interesting fact that Matthew shares. The crowd responds to Pilate placing the blame on them by saying, "Let his blood be on us and our children." I shudder at this. Not only are the people accepting their culpability in Jesus's murder, but they also afflict their children with their guilt. What a burden for them, even though it wasn't the children's decision.

Yet aren't we all to blame? We have all sinned and need Jesus to save us. Doesn't this also make us responsible for his death?

Questions: *Before we place blame for Jesus's death on Herod, Pilate, the religious leaders, and the mob, how should we view our role? Does God speak to us in dreams, like Pilate's wife? Why or why not?*

Prayer: Jesus, we confess our sins to you and follow you as our Savior.

DAY 39, SATURDAY: JESUS MOCKED

TODAY'S PASSAGE: MATTHEW 27:27–31, MARK 14:65, 15:16–20, LUKE 22:63–65, AND JOHN 19:1–5

Focus verse: *After they had mocked him, they took off the robe and put his own clothes on him. Then they led him away to crucify him.* (Matthew 27:31)

After Pilate releases Barabbas, he has Jesus flogged and hands him over to his soldiers to crucify him.

A whole troop gathers round Jesus. They're going to have some fun. They strip him of his clothes and put a royal robe on him. This isn't out of respect, as we'll soon see, but ridicule.

They make a crown out of thorns and put it on his head. But don't assume they do this gently.

Certainly, they use as much force as they can, to produce the greatest pain—and the most blood.

They give him a staff to hold as a pretend scepter and bow before him. The soldiers mockingly taunt, "Hail, king of the Jews!" They spit on him and strike his head with the staff they've given him—over and over.

Mark and Luke add that the soldiers blindfold and beat him, demanding that he prophesy who hit him. Luke also reports that they say "many other insulting things to him."

When they tire of their sport, they remove the robe and put his clothes back on.

This, however, isn't the first time people mock him during his ordeal. Herod and his soldiers already tormented him (Day 36).

And it won't be the last. As we'll soon see, Jesus receives ridicule from the people watching and walking by as he hangs on the cross dying (Matthew 27:39–44, Mark 15:29–32, and Luke 23:35–37).

Some of those people wrongly recall his statement about destroying the temple and rebuilding it three days later (Day 31). "Save yourself!" they urge. "If you're really God's Son, come down from the cross—then maybe we'll believe you." The religious leaders are also there to taunt him.

Part of me wants to see Jesus vindicate himself. He could do that. He already said he could ask Papa for twelve legions of angels to defend him (Matthew 26:53). They'd preserve his honor and strike the mockers dead. But Jesus doesn't do that. Without retaliating against his tormentors, he opts to see his mission through.

We see this prophesied in the book of Psalms. "All who see me mock me; they hurl insults, shaking their heads." (Psalm 22:7).

Jesus himself also foresaw that this would happen. We see this the third time he predicted his death (Day 3). Speaking about himself in the third person, Jesus said that they will mock him, insult him, spit on him, flog him, and kill him (Luke 18:32–33).

Questions: *When we're hurt or wronged, how do we know when to stand up for ourselves and when to turn it over to God? Whether in big ways or small, how have we mocked God, either directly or indirectly?*

Prayer: Jesus, thank you for seeing your mission through and dying to save us.

DAY 40, SUNDAY: SIMON FROM CYRENE

TODAY'S PASSAGE: MATTHEW 27:32, MARK 15:21, AND LUKE 23:26

Focus verse: *They met a man from Cyrene, named Simon, and they forced him to carry the cross.* (Matthew 27:32)

At this point Jesus has been flogged and had thorns driven into his head. He's been slapped, hit repeatedly with fists, and struck many times with a stick. He's been physically abused, and his condition is awful.

Despite this, the Roman soldiers expect Jesus to carry his cross to his place of execution. History says this was the usual practice for victims facing crucifixion. John tells us Jesus was able to carry his cross all the way to the place of the skull, Golgotha (John 19:17).

Matthew, Mark, and Luke, however, tell us that Jesus can't drag his own cross the full distance. In his weakened state, from the beatings and abuse heaped upon him, he can't make it. The soldiers certainly don't want to lug this weighty instrument of death through the city streets. As an alternative, they grab someone from the crowd and force him to do it.

The man's name is Simon and he's from Cyrene. He's in the wrong place at the wrong time.

Archeologists tell us that ancient Cyrene was along the coast of northern Africa, in modern-day Libya. What's Simon doing so far from home? Given that it's Passover, we suspect he's coming into the city for the celebration. This would mean that Simon from Cyrene is Jewish or a convert to Judaism.

Other than knowing where Simon comes from and that he's a victim of bad timing, we know one more thing about him. He has two boys: Alexander and Rufus. Mark may share this detail because his audience knows Alexander and Rufus, but this is only conjecture (consider Acts 19:33 and Romans 16:13).

As far as Simon from Cyrene is concerned, he only appears in these three verses when he carries the cross for Jesus. Aside from these things, we know nothing else about him from Scripture.

Though he's forced to do so, Simon is the first person to help Jesus after his arrest. Does he see his forced labor as a service to Jesus, or as helping the Roman soldiers end the life of a man the Jewish leaders view as a troublemaker, heretic, and blasphemer?

We also don't know what happens to Simon after he carries Jesus's cross for him. Is Simon's life changed because of his brief encounter with Jesus? Does he feel guilt for his unwilling role in bringing about the death of an innocent man?

Perhaps Simon ends up following Jesus. We can hope so.

Questions: *How do we respond when we're forced to do something? What is a pivotal point in your life when your future could have gone in one of two directions, like Simon after he carried Jesus's cross?*

Prayer: Jesus, show us how we can serve you—and do so willingly.

DAY 41, MONDAY: GOLGOTHA

TODAY'S PASSAGE: MATTHEW 27:33–36, MARK 15:22–25, LUKE 23:27–31, AND JOHN 19:17–18, 23–27

Focus verse: *They came to a place called Golgotha.* (Matthew 27:33)

The Roman soldiers lead Jesus, along with Simon from Cyrene carrying his cross, to Golgotha. Golgotha means "the place of the skull," no doubt referencing it as a spot of death and befitting an execution. Having completed what the soldiers forced him to do, we can imagine Simon from Cyrene scooting away the first chance he gets. Or does he stay to see what happens?

It is there, at Golgotha, that the Roman soldiers crucify Jesus.

They strip him of his clothes and divide it

among themselves, one fourth for each of them. Rather than cut his seamless undergarment into four pieces, they cast lots to see who gets it, just as prophesied centuries earlier in Psalm 22:18.

They offer him wine mixed with gall or myrrh —perhaps a concoction to dull the pain. Considering the brutality of crucifixion, offering a mild painkiller seems out of place. After tasting it and realizing what it is, Jesus refuses any more. It's as if he needs to bear the full agony himself.

Many people follow him there, including women who mourn and wail for him. Jesus tells them not to weep for him, but to weep for themselves and their children. This alludes to his earlier prophecy in Matthew 24:19. He also quotes from Isaiah 2:19 and Hosea 10:8.

Near the cross stand his mother, his aunt, Mary the wife of Clopas, and Mary Magdalene. The disciple Jesus loved—John—is there too. Jesus says to Mary, "Here is your son." And to John he says, "Here is your mother." From that moment on, John takes Mary into his own home.

We may wonder why Jesus doesn't tell one of his brothers—James, Joseph, Simon, or Judas—to do this. It might be they weren't present or didn't yet believe in him (John 7:5) and he wants his mother's care to go to someone who does.

It is the third hour of the day—9 a.m. The soldiers sit down to keep watch over Jesus. They must make sure he dies and that someone doesn't remove him from the cross before he does.

Questions: *Who can we be with during their time of need? How can we better care for our family and friends?*

Prayer: Lord, may we care for others in their time of need.

DAY 42, TUESDAY: THE KING OF THE JEWS

TODAY'S PASSAGE: MATTHEW 27:37, MARK 15:26, LUKE 23:38, AND JOHN 19:19–22

Focus verse: *Above his head they placed the written charge against him: this is Jesus, the king of the Jews.* (Matthew 27:37)

A t this point in our narrative, Matthew notes that the charge against Jesus, placed above his head on the cross, is "This is Jesus, the king of the Jews." Mark and Luke are even more concise, but John gives more details.

John shares that Pilate has this information posted about Jesus. It says, "Jesus of Nazareth, the King of the Jews." The sign appears in three languages: Aramaic, Latin, and Greek. This should allow all who pass by to read it in a language they know.

The Jewish leaders should be content that Jesus is about to die, yet they find a reason to complain. They go to Pilate and say, "Don't write 'the King of the Jews,' but that this man *claimed* to be king of the Jews."

Pilate says, "I've written what I've written."

When Pilate asked Jesus if he was a king, Jesus agreed. Jesus, however, never called himself the king of the Jews. And though others—including Satan and demons—refer to him as the Son of God, Jesus calls himself the Son of Man. This may be to emphasize his human nature (Son of Man) contrasted to his divine nature (Son of God).

It is Pilate who calls Jesus the King of the Jews. This may be his conclusion after interrogating Jesus (Matthew 27:11). Those who mock Jesus follow Pilate's lead in calling him the king of the Jews (Matthew 27:29).

Yet Pilate isn't the first person to refer to Jesus as the king of the Jews. Recall some three decades earlier when the Magi arrive searching for baby Jesus. They ask King Herod, "Where is the baby born king of the Jews?" (Matthew 2:1–2). Though the Magi aren't Jewish, their research after seeing the star in the sky leads them to conclude that the baby is king, the king of the Jews.

The Old Testament prophesies that the coming Savior will be a king (Jeremiah 23:5 and Zechariah 9:9). And when Jesus makes his triumphant entry into Jerusalem riding a foal, the people praise him as a king (Luke 19:38 and John 12:13; see Day 6).

Yet most of Jesus's own people don't see him as king.

Questions: *Is Jesus your king? If not, how do you view him? What do you think about Jesus referring to himself as the Son of Man and not the Son of God?*

Prayer: Jesus, may we celebrate you as king, the Son of God, the Son of Man—and our Savior.

DAY 43, WEDNESDAY: TWO REBELS

TODAY'S PASSAGE: MATTHEW 27:38, MARK
15:27, LUKE 23:32–33, 39–43, AND JOHN 19:18

Focus verse: *Two rebels were crucified with him.*
(Matthew 27:38)

We commonly think of two thieves or robbers crucified on either side of Jesus. Yet history tells us that the Romans didn't crucify people for stealing. Crucifixion was a capital punishment for capital offenses.

Though the most common labels for these two men in the various translations of the Bible are robbers and thieves, other versions, including the NIV, use rebels. We also see other translations

PETER DEHAAN

calling them criminals and revolutionaries. These last three labels—rebels, criminals, and revolution-aries—stand as a more historically correct under-standing of this passage.

Some Bible scholars think the two rebels cruci-fied along with Jesus took part in the same insurrec-tion as Barabbas. They may even align themselves with the Zealots. We can speculate that the three crosses were for Barabbas and his two coconspira-tors. But when Pilate released Barabbas that left one cross available. They used that cross to execute Jesus. In this scenario, Jesus dies in place of Barabbas. This, of course, is all conjecture and goes beyond the biblical text.

Another reasonable assumption is that both rebels are Jewish. Since their execution takes place in Jerusalem, that's likely where they committed their crimes and near where they live. It's unlikely that non-Jews would travel to Jerusalem to rebel against the Roman government.

Matthew and Mark will later note that the two rebels join in with all the others in insulting Jesus. Luke, however, clarifies that only one rebel mocks Jesus.

He writes that one criminal insults him, saying "If you're the Messiah, save yourself and us!"

But the second criminal rebukes the first. "Don't you fear God? We deserve our punishment for what we did, but this man did nothing wrong." He directs his attention to Jesus. "Remember me when you come into your kingdom."

In one of the most comforting of responses, Jesus replies, "I promise that today you'll join me in paradise." This makes the rebel crucified next to Jesus the very first person Jesus saves.

All this man did was affirm his guilt and ask Jesus to remember him in death. For Jesus, that's enough, and he promises salvation to this rebel being executed for capital offenses.

We must consider this simple and delightful redemption story to reform our theology about salvation. Most people make salvation much more complicated than Jesus intended when he said, "follow me" (Luke 9:23). The rebel on the cross— who makes a deathbed confession and receives Jesus's affirmation—proves this.

Questions: *What do you think about the rebel's salvation experience? What assumptions about salvation have you heard that you might need to rethink in view of what the Bible teaches?*

Prayer: Jesus, may we not add extra requirements on how to be saved and instead follow you as you instructed.

DAY 44, THURSDAY: THE SEVEN LAST SAYINGS OF JESUS ON THE CROSS

TODAY'S PASSAGE: MATTHEW 27:39–46

Focus verse: *Jesus cried out in a loud voice, "Eli, Eli, lema sabachthani?" (which means "My God, my God, why have you forsaken me?").* (Matthew 27:46)

Jesus dies an excruciating death on the cross. He's hung there for six hours, though his torment started much earlier in the day. At one point he calls out in agony to his Father in heaven, "My God, why are you forsaking me?"

Remember what happens in Day 30 after Jesus's arrest? All his disciples abandon him, but Father God stays with him—until now. Jesus came to earth to die for our sins. This includes the past, present, and future sins of all people throughout history. Jesus must do this one thing alone.

With this in mind, we can envision Father God turning his head aside for a moment so Jesus can complete his task on his own without divine intervention to lessen the collective weight of humanity's sins. He must bear this alone. That's when he cries out to his Father.

These are the only dying words of Jesus that Matthew and Mark record, while Luke and John give us other things Jesus says on the cross. In total, these four writers document seven things Jesus says as he dies.

Here are the seven last sayings of Jesus on the cross:

1. **"Father, forgive them, for they don't know what they're doing"** (Luke 23:34). Jesus models forgiveness. He teaches that if we don't forgive others, God won't forgive us (Matthew 6:15).

Stephen, the Bible's first martyr, does this as the mob stones him to death. He asks God to not hold his attackers accountable and to forgive them (Acts 7:60).

2. To the rebel crucified next to him, Jesus promises that they'll spend eternity together.

"Truly I tell you, today you'll be with me in paradise" (Luke 23:43; Day 43).

3. As Jesus dies, he feels concern for his mother. He asks John to care for her. Jesus says to Mary, **"Here's your son,"** and to the disciple, **"Here's your mother"** (John 19:26–27; Day 41).

Jesus, in his deepest despair, still thinks of others. We should do the same.

4. As we mentioned, Jesus must complete this journey on his own. He calls out, **"God, why have you forsaken me?"** (Matthew 27:46 and Mark 15:34). This fulfills David's prophetic words in Psalm 22:1.

Though it's necessary for Jesus to do this on his own, we never need do anything by ourselves. God is always with us and will never forsake us (Hebrews 13:5, quoting Deuteronomy 31:6, 8).

5. Being thirsty while undergoing one of history's most brutal forms of execution is minor compared to all else Jesus physically endures. Though no one can help him deal with any of those sufferings, someone can give him a drink.

This may be why he says, **"I'm thirsty"** (John 19:28). We see this foreshadowed by David (Psalm 22:15). Earlier Jesus taught his followers to give water to those in need (Matthew 10:42).

6. As Jesus is about to die, he will fulfill what he came to earth to do. He confirms this when he tells everyone keeping vigil, **"It is finished"** (John 19:30).

7. Death completes Jesus's earthly mission. Rather than suffer any longer, he wills himself to die and gives his spirit over to Papa: **"Father, into your hands I commit my spirit"** (Luke 23:46). This fulfills David's prophetic words in Psalm 31:5.

Questions: Which of these things that Jesus says means the most to you? Which one deserves greater consideration?

Prayer: Jesus, may we receive these words—and all your words—as your message to us.

DAY 45, FRIDAY: THE DEATH OF JESUS

TODAY'S PASSAGE: MATTHEW 27:45–54, MARK 15:33–39, LUKE 23:44–48, AND JOHN 19:28–30

Focus verse: *When Jesus had cried out again in a loud voice, he gave up his spirit.* (Matthew 27:50)

When Jesus cries out "Eli, Eli, lema sabachthani?", some people think he's calling for Elijah. They're curious. They want to see if Elijah shows up. (He doesn't.)

Yet someone else runs to get a sponge filled with wine vinegar. John writes that this is because Jesus says, "I'm thirsty." The person offers the sponge to Jesus, and Luke says he drinks it.

Luke also says that darkness covers the area for

three hours, from noon until three. It is indeed a dark time, exposing the depravity of humanity's sins and placing them on Jesus's shoulders for him alone to bear.

He gives his spirit over to God and proclaims, "It is finished."

At that he takes his final breath.

Jesus is dead.

He dies in our place on the cross, serving as the ultimate sin sacrifice to end all sin sacrifices. In doing so, he fulfills what he came to do, what he told his disciples would happen (Day 1 and Day 3).

Three things occur at his death. Matthew covers all three, with Mark and Luke corroborating with more details.

First, the curtain in the temple rips from top to bottom. This suggests that God initiated the split from above, something no person could do while standing on the ground. This symbolizes that, because of Jesus's death, all people can now enter the holy of holies and approach God directly. They no longer need a priest to serve as their intermediary.

Next, an earthquake occurs, and tombs break open. The bodies of many holy people rise to life.

We don't know who they are or how many, only that they lived holy lives. Were they martyred for their faith? Did they live in faithful expectation of Jesus? How long had they been dead?

Regardless, after Jesus's resurrection, they come out of their tombs, go into Jerusalem, and appear to many people. What an amazing sight this must have been, the dead raised to life. Because of Jesus's death, they are alive again. After the rebel on the cross, these resurrected individuals, in a sense, are the next group of people Jesus rescues.

Third, the centurion who sees what happens—along with the guards standing watch—says, "Surely he was the Son of God!" What a profound testimony, and from a non-Jew, a nonbeliever. We can hope the experience forever changed the centurion.

Luke adds that all the people who gathered to witness Jesus's death mourn his passing as they leave.

Questions: *What do you think about the things that happened when Jesus died? Which of the details of Jesus's death most affects you? Why?*

Prayer: Jesus, thank you for loving us so much that you died in our place for our sins to make us right with Father God.

EPILOGUE: HE HAS RISEN

TODAY'S PASSAGE: MATTHEW 28:1–10

Focus verse: *"He is not here; he has risen, just as he said."* (Matthew 28:6)

Jesus dies, but this isn't the end. In many respects, it's the beginning.

After he dies, he's buried.

Three days later, he rises from the dead. We call this Easter when we celebrate his resurrection from his tomb. A better label—which also avoids the secularization of Easter—is Resurrection Sunday.

On this first Resurrection Sunday, Jesus is victorious over the finality of death. This proves his mastery over the grave. Through his resurrection power that he provides, we, too, can rise from the dead. And if we follow Jesus, we will. Then we'll live with him and Father God forever.

Thank you, Jesus.

Questions: *What does Jesus's death mean to you? What about Jesus's resurrection?*

Prayer: Jesus, may we cherish your victory over death when you rose from the dead.

Continue the story and explore what happens next in *The Victory of Jesus* (an Easter devotional), book three in the *Holiday Celebration Devotionals*.

If you liked *The Passion of Jesus*, please leave a review online. Your review will help others discover this book and encourage them to read it too.

Thank you.

BOOKS IN THE HOLIDAY DEVOTIONALS SERIES

Which devotional do you want to read next?

- The Advent of Jesus
- The Victory of Jesus (Easter)
- The Ministry of Jesus
- Thanksgiving with Jesus
- New Year with Jesus

Be the first to hear about Peter's new books and receive updates at PeterDeHaan.com/updates.

IF YOU'RE NEW TO THE BIBLE

Each entry in this book contains Bible references. These can guide you if you want to learn more. If you're not familiar with the Bible, here's an overview to get you started, give some context, and minimize confusion.

First, the Bible is a collection of works written by various authors over several centuries. Think of the Bible as a diverse anthology of godly communication. It contains historical accounts, poetry, songs, letters of instruction and encouragement, messages from God sent through his representatives, and prophecies.

Most versions of the Bible have sixty-six books grouped into two sections: The Old Testament and the New Testament. The Old Testament contains thirty-nine books that precede and anticipate Jesus. The New Testament includes twenty-seven books and covers Jesus's life and the work of his followers.

The reference notations in the Bible, such as Romans 3:23, are analogous to line numbers in a Shakespearean play. They serve as a study aid. Since the Bible is much longer and more complex than a play, its reference notations are more involved.

As already mentioned, the Bible is an amalgam of books, or sections, such as Genesis, Matthew, or Acts. These are the names given to them, over time, based on the piece's author, audience, or purpose.

In the 1200s, each book was divided into chapters, such as Acts 2 or Psalm 23. In the 1500s, the chapters were further subdivided into verses, such as John 3:16. Let's use this as an example.

The name of the book (John) appears first, followed by the chapter number (3), a colon, and then the verse number (16). Sometimes called a chapter-verse reference notation, this helps people quickly find a specific text regardless of their version of the Bible.

Although the goal was to place these chapter and verse divisions at logical breaks, they sometimes seem arbitrary. Therefore, it's good practice to read what precedes and follows each passage you're studying. The text before or after it may contain relevant insights into the portion you're exploring.

Here's how to look up a specific passage in the Bible based on its reference: Most Bibles contain a table of contents, which gives the page number for the beginning of each book. Start there. Locate the book you want to read, and turn to that page. Then flip forward to the chapter you want. Last, skim that chapter to locate the specific verse.

If you want to read online, enter the reference into BibleGateway.com or BibleHub.com. Also check out the YouVersion app.

Learn more about the greatest book ever written at ABibleADay.com, which provides a Bible blog, summaries of the books of the Bible, a dictionary of Bible terms, Bible reading plans, and other resources.

ABOUT PETER DEHAAN

Peter DeHaan, PhD, wants to change the world one word at a time. His books and blog posts discuss God, the Bible, and church, geared toward spiritual seekers and church dropouts. Many people feel church has let them down, and Peter seeks to encourage them as they search for a place to belong.

But he's not afraid to ask tough questions or make religious people squirm. He's not trying to be provocative. Instead, he seeks truth, even if it makes people uncomfortable. Peter urges Christians to push past the status quo and reexamine how they practice their faith in every part of their lives.

Peter earned his doctorate, awarded with high distinction, from Trinity College of the Bible and Theological Seminary. He lives with his wife in beautiful Southwest Michigan and wrangles cross-word puzzles in his spare time.

A lifelong student of Scripture, Peter wrote the 1,000-page website ABibleADay.com to encourage people to explore the Bible, the greatest book ever written. His popular blog addresses biblical Christianity to build a faith that matters.

Read his blog, receive his newsletter, and learn more at PeterDeHaan.com.

BOOKS BY PETER DEHAAN

Holiday Celebration Devotionals

The Advent of Jesus

The Passion of Jesus (Lent)

The Victory of Jesus (Easter)

The Ministry of Jesus

Thanksgiving with Jesus

New Year with Jesus

40-Day Bible Study Series

Dear Theophilus (the Gospel of Luke)

Acts Bible Study

Isaiah Bible Study

Minor Prophets Bible Study

Job Bible Study

Living Water (John)

Love Is Patient (1 and 2 Corinthians)

Revelation Bible Study

1, 2, & 3 John Bible Study

Hebrews Bible Study

James and Jude Bible Study

Matthew Bible Study

1 & 2 Peter Bible Study

Mark Bible Study

Bible Character Sketches Series

Women of the Bible

The Friends and Foes of Jesus

Old Testament Sinners and Saints

More Old Testament Sinners and Saints

Heroes and Heavies of the Apocrypha

200 Old Testament Sinners and Saints

Visiting Churches Series

52 Churches

The 52 Churches Workbook

More Than 52 Churches

The More Than 52 Churches Workbook

Visiting Online Church

Other Books

Elephant God

Jesus's Broken Church

Martin Luther's 95 Theses (formerly *95 Tweets*)

The Christian Church's LGBTQ Failure

Bridging the Sacred-Secular Divide (formerly *Woodpecker Wars*)

Beyond Psalm 150

How Big Is Your Tent?

For the latest list of all Peter's books, go to PeterDeHaan.com/books.